On Target
Englisch für Auffrischungskurse

Teacher's Book

von
Christine Frank
Jenny Richardson-Schlötter

D1725787

Ernst Klett Verlag für Wissen und Bildung
Stuttgart · Dresden

On Target
Teacher's Book

von
Christine Frank
Jenny Richardson-Schlötter

Einbandgestaltung:
Hanjo Schmidt

Gedruckt auf umweltfreundlichem Recyclingpapier, gefertigt aus 100 % Altpapier

1. Auflage   1 ⁴ ³ ² ¹ | 1997 96 95 94

Alle Drucke dieser Auflage können im Unterricht nebeneinander benutzt werden.
Die letzte Zahl bezeichnet das Jahr dieses Druckes.

Redaktion: Margit Duda, Caroline Haydon
Druck: F. + W. Schmidt, Renningen. Printed in Germany.
ISBN 3-12-560811-2

Contents

Symbols and abbreviations

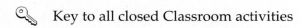 Key to all closed Classroom activities

i Cultural information and language notes

☞ Teacher's note

C1B/2 = Classroom, Unit 1, B-Block, exercise 2

H2C/3 = Home study, Unit 2, C-Block, exercise 3

***On Target* consists of:**

Student's Book: Klett-Nr. 560810

Teacher's Book: Klett-Nr. 560811

2 Cassettes: Klett-Nr. 560812

2 CDs: Klett-Nr. 560813

Introduction

1. General concept of *On Target*

Target Group

On Target is a refresher course for adult learners at Volkshochschulen and other language schools. It leads in one volume to the level of the VHS-/ICC-Certificate.

The course is designed to cater for learners with varied previous learning experience who all have a relatively well-founded, if somewhat heterogenous, knowledge of English which they can draw on.

Such course participants will, as a rule, be familiar with the foreign language learning process, i.e. acquainted with certain learning techniques and strategies, and will be intent on reactivating their knowledge of English within a short period of time.

Overview of timing and distribution of material

Year	Semester	Units
1	1	1–5
	2	6–10

→ VHS-/ICC-Certificate English

Coursebook components

On Target consists of the following:

• Student's Book with integrated Home study section, Map of the book, Units 1–10, Review, Reading for fun.
Appendix: Files, Grammar, Key (Home study section), Tapescripts, Vocabulary, Tips and books.

• Audio material: 2 Cassettes/CDs
The listening texts on the cassettes and CDs are identical.

• Teacher's Book with explanations of general concept, unit-for-unit descriptions of procedure, solutions to all tasks in the Classroom section, photocopiable teaching materials.

Didactic concept

On Target combines material for work in the classroom and for self study at home. Successful learning will depend on consistent attention to the Home study section, which is designed as an integral, obligatory component of the course. *On Target* is based on a communicative-functional approach, with the four skills being integrated from the very start. While the Classroom section gives priority to the training of productive skills, the Home study section concentrates primarily on the development of receptive skills.

Structure and timing of the course

On Target is divided into 10 units providing material for a total of 30 double lessons (45 hours) in the classroom and the equivalent of 45 hours self study at home.
Each unit – except for Unit 10 – covers 20 pages. Of these, six pages (organized as doublespread pages) are devoted to classroom work and 12 pages to self study. The remaining two pages of each unit consist of a one-page review and a page of reading for fun.
The units are illustrated in colour and have a clear and consistent structure. Each unit in the Classroom section and in the Home study section is subdivided into three blocks: A, B and C. Each block represents a double lesson (90 minutes) in the classroom and a further 90 minutes of independent self study. Each A-, B- or C-Block of the Home study section follows on directly and is thematically linked to the corresponding A-, B- or C-Block of the Classroom section.
The C-Blocks of the Classroom and Home study section in Unit 10 are exceptions in that they do not contain the usual unit-specific exercises. Instead, in both sections of the unit, this block consists of a game which picks up on things learnt throughout the course, providing a fun way of reviewing and revising the course as a whole.
Apart from information on Great Britain, USA and other English-speaking countries the themes in *On Target* are derived from private and public everyday life (e.g. People, Places, Food, Free time, Travel, Home and environment, etc.).

Overview of the timing of a unit

	1st week	Time	2nd week	Time	3rd week	Time	Total
Classroom	A-Block	1 double lesson = 90 mins	B-Block	1 double lesson = 90 mins	C-Block	1 double lesson = 90 mins	3 double lessons = 4 ½ hours
Home study	A-Block	90 mins	B-Block	90 mins	C-Block	90 mins	4 ½ hours

Review

The review page offers a survey of the most important language items, both communicative and structural, dealt with in that particular unit.

It contains, for example, a summary of the major language functions dealt with in the unit together with their exponents as well as references to all places in the book where these are encountered.

This is followed by a summary of the grammatical structures practised in the unit, with cross-references to the grammar section in the appendix of the coursebook.

The structures in each unit are listed in the order in which they occur in the A-, B- and C-Blocks. At the end of each review page there is a so-called *Tip* listing a range of ideas – in terms of the four skills – of how learners can optimize their individual learning progress.

Reading for fun

In addition to the reading texts within each unit, which are primarily oriented to reading skills development, each unit is also rounded off with a page of reading for fun. This contains a varied collection of texts (e.g. rhymes, poems, proverbs, limericks, recipes, cartoons, etc.) relating to the theme of that particular unit. The texts are usually quite amusing, the main aim being to promote enjoyment of reading in the target language.

Grammar

Grammar in *On Target* aims to help the learner use certain grammatical structures actively in communication. This communicative-functional approach to the treatment of grammar means that there is no specific focus on grammar in the lessons.

At this level it is assumed that learners know the basic grammatical structures of English, so that emphasis is primarily placed on revision of important structures.

The Classroom section has a relatively shallow progression. It concentrates on recycling the structures which are frequently used in communicative contexts (e.g. *present simple* and *past simple*).

The Home study section, in addition to providing revision and consolidation of all the structures dealt with in the Classroom section, also contains tasks which call for more complex grammar either not touched on at all or referred to only marginally in the Classroom section. Here the learners are invited to reactivate their knowledge of English in self study and to consolidate this knowledge in situative language contexts.

Although the emphasis in *On Target* is clearly on the use of language (skills development, vocabulary growth), this does not mean that a systematic and comprehensible presentation of grammar is lacking. The appendix of the coursebook contains exactly this sort of grammar survey, which can be referred to for explanation at any time during the lessons. Since the rules are presented in German and illustrated with a range of English-German example sentences, the grammar also represents a particularly useful reference in combination with the self-study tasks in the Home study section.

Language practice

On Target contains a wide variety of tasks designed not only to appeal to various learner types but also to constantly encourage the learners to make active use of the target language. In addition, the exercises in *On Target* vary in terms of how challenging they are, so that the full range of learner needs in a heterogenous refresher group are catered for.

In keeping with the different priorities of the Classroom section and the Home study section in terms of skills training, some activities in the lessons concentrate on the careful use of language and focus mainly on accuracy whereas in others students develop fluency through freer, more creative use of language.
The tasks provided range from highly controlled and less-controlled forms – mostly still guided by means of linguistic cues (e.g. speech bubbles, example sentences, model dialogues, flow diagrams, etc.) – to relatively free production activities involving communicative situations which could prove useful for the learner in everyday life.

The Home study section contains numerous exercises for the revision, consolidation and expansion of work done in class and respects the needs of a heterogenous learning group.
The main types of exercise are matching and combination tasks, jumbled sentences, true / false activities, gap-filling exercises, picture-cued tasks, learning games (crossword puzzles, quizzes), definition tasks and word-grouping tasks based on personal associations (e.g. mind maps).

Apart from tasks which aim to expand and consolidate structures and vocabulary, the Home study section also contains a number of comprehension activities designed to systematically train reading and listening skills.

Skills

On Target employs a variety of approaches to ensure systematic training in the four skills.

Speaking: A central aim in *On Target* is the promotion of oral communication ability in everyday situations.

Learners are constantly encouraged to use language communicatively (e.g. to structure dialogues, to familiarize themselves with and to make use of conversational strategies, to perform role plays, to express personal opinions, etc.). Although such activities are often controlled in terms of form, they are designed to allow plenty of room for individual creativity in terms of content. They have a speculative character which stimulates the learners to think and speak.

Listening: Listening comprehension skills in *On Target* are developed systematically through a range of specific activities.

The pre-listening stage requires the learner to do certain tasks before listening to the text (e.g. predicting information, answering questions, completing gapped texts, filling in diagrams or charts).

The post-listening stage takes place after the cassette or CD has been played. Here, listening comprehension is being tested rather than practised (e.g. true/false discrimination; gap-texts with choices for completion; matching tasks; jumbled sentences, etc.).

The listening comprehension activities in the Home study section are usually relatively short, with tasks which involve answering questions, taking over a part in a conversation, or ticking what was heard.

The listening texts in the Classroom section consist of longer interviews, conversations, reports, etc., and are therefore more demanding.

Reading: *On Target* contains a range of British and American reading texts, some of them authentic, others adapted. Here special care has been taken to ensure a wide variety of text types. As well as narratives and dialogues, there are texts in the form of letters, songs, notes, small ads, brochures, maps, crossword puzzles, newspaper articles, etc. Reading, like listening, calls for information to be processed. The various tasks aim at familiarizing the learners with specific reading strategies (e.g. reading for information, reading for specific information), thus enabling them to read the texts as they would in their own native language.

Texts which are beyond the level of the learners in terms of grammar and lexis are not intended for detailed comprehension. Such texts are accompanied by carefully graded tasks designed to make understanding easier and more manageable for the learners.

Writing: Writing practice is primarily provided in the Home study section, usually taking the form of controlled writing activities. These are complemented by freer writing activities in the Classroom section, where learners are frequently required to take notes (note taking), or to prepare texts to present to the class orally using cue words (note making) which they can then use as memory aids during their presentations.

Forms of interaction

An important feature of *On Target* is the intentional change in forms of interaction according to the various types of practice activity. The main criterion for the choice of a specific interaction form is always what is most appropriate for the learners and for the particular target language being dealt with.

The coursebook therefore contains a balanced range of interaction forms including individual, pair- and groupwork as well as role play.

Pairwork offers the learners the chance to try out new language before presenting results to the whole class, and provides an effective means of practising dialogues. Psychologically, pairwork activities prove to be less stressful for the learner because he/she is only faced with one person to speak to.
Groupwork in *On Target*, as an extended form of pairwork, usually consists of several clearly organized stages, each with precise instructions.

Role play activities address the learners directly and invite them to make creative use of the language they have acquired. As in pair- and groupwork sequences, there are specific instructions for role plays, but these allow much more room for autonomous decisions concerning the content or form of the communication.

Vocabulary

The lexis encountered in *On Target* consists of more than the vocabulary which learners are expected to use actively by the end of the course. Learners are supposed to acquire a core vocabulary of words contained in the *VHS-Certificate* wordlist. They are also given the opportunity to learn additional vocabulary if they wish. The alphabetical English-German glossary assumes knowledge of lexical items in the *Waystage* catalogue. Words listed here belong to *VHS-Certificate* vocabulary. It also features key items from listening texts and from those reading texts where the intention is not primarily to encourage reading strategies.

A refresher learner's vocabulary is more than merely the sum of all the lexical items learnt in previous courses. It also involves a system of relationships and networks (e.g. lexical fields, collocation fields) which not only support retention and speedy recall of words but also aid understanding of as yet unknown lexis.
For this reason *On Target* makes sure that even the vocabulary which is assumed as known (cf. *Waystage* list) is consistently consolidated in new connections and contexts.

In addition to the recycling and consolidation of already known words, *On Target* attaches great importance to vocabulary expansion (contextually networked vocabulary learning) and to the fostering of learner autonomy in terms of strategic responses to foreign language lexis. This is provided through a range of activities, e.g. gap-filling exercises, matching tasks, picture-cued tasks, crossword puzzles, quizzes, definition tasks, exercises on word families and lexical fields, exercises on lexical relationships (collocations), word-building tasks and paraphrase tasks.

Audio material for the course

The listening material for *On Target* consists of two cassettes / two CDs which are absolutely essential for work in the classroom and for work at home. They contain recordings for all the activities marked with the cassette symbol ▣. Tapescripts of the recordings can be found in the appendix of the Student's Book (pages 256–275). They often serve as keys to the tasks. On the cassettes / CDs the listening texts are identified by two acoustic signals: a deep tone (a synthesizer) for the Classroom section and a high-pitched tone (a triangle) for the Home study section.
British and American native speakers were used for the recordings so that learners can familiarize themselves with the range of phonological variations in spoken English. With regard to the differences in vocabulary and spelling in British and American English, the American texts have been kept in the original in order to maintain the authenticity of the language. In the accompanying activities, however, British English is used throughout.

2. Using *On Target* in the Classroom

The Teacher's Book is designed to help you make the most appropriate use of the Classroom section with your students. The structure of the Teacher's Book follows the same principle as the Student's Book, i.e. each A-, B- or C-Block of the Classroom section is directly followed by the corresponding A-, B- or C-Block of the Home study section.

It is very important to introduce your students to the Home study section at the first class meeting and to explain how to use it. Check every week whether the students are keeping up with the Home study exercises or whether they have any problems. You can do this at the beginning of class by walking around and looking at the students' work. Students can and should, of course, correct their own work using the key in the back of the book, but it is very motivating for them to see that their work is being noticed and taken seriously. Remind the students that it is absolutely essential to work through the Home study section continuously and systematically in order to make progress.

Extra vs. further activities

On Target offers you additional material which can be used to individualize your teaching. There are *extra activities* in the Classroom section that occasionally occur at the end of the A-, B- or C-Block. The intention of these activities is to provide supplementary material for classes or individual students who work faster.

As opposed to the *extra activities*, you will find a section of *further activities* for classroom use at the back of the Teacher's Book on pages 109-117. This is purely optional material. The activities focus on using the language in different situative contexts by revising vocabulary, functions and grammar either practised in the Classroom or the Home study section.

You will find material for individual work, for pair- or groupwork, for large and small classes, for classes that are better/weaker than average, etc. There are also a number of photocopiable worksheets with role plays, conversation activities and vocabulary exercises accompanying some of the *further activities* to suit the individual needs of your students.

Partner-finding activities

At the back of the Teacher's Book on pages 128-133 you will find six different sets of photocopiable card games for regrouping students. The activities are very much vocabulary based and recycle a great deal of language students have come across in *On Target*.

Each card game consists of 28 individual cards. Every student is given a card and asked to find the person whose card matches their own. After they have completed the task you might want to ask them to extend the activity by finding further examples. Finally, ask the students to read out their matching cards. The newly found examples can be collected on the board or OHP.

The order in which the cards are arranged on the photocopiable worksheets provides the matching answers and can therefore be regarded as the key to the activities. Make sure that you shuffle the cards well before you distribute them among the students.

Overview of the Classroom section, Teacher's Book

Unit 1 · People

Classroom A

Students learn each others' names and something about one another.

Functions	introducing oneself and each other; reacting to introduction *(Hello,) I'm … / This is … / Nice to meet you.*
Grammar	present simple *(to be)*
Skills	speaking: exchange of information about each other reading: reading sentences to decide which information is relevant listening: listening for information

☞ During the first lesson you should make sure the students understand the importance of the Home study section. It is intended to reinforce and expand material worked on in class. Draw the students' attention also to the review pages, the reading for fun and the appendix.

Procedure

1 Get the students to form groups according to the number of letters in their name. They introduce themselves to everybody in their group.

Then get them to form groups according to the number of syllables in their name and to introduce themselves or each other.
If you have a group of more than 15 students you can get them to form groups according to the initial letter of their name.

ⓘ In Britain and America the use of first names is common among groups working or socializing together.

2 a Tell the students to read the sentences in File 1, page 210, and to write down only those sentences that are true for them.

File 1 (page 210)

> 1. I know some of the other people in this class.
> 2. I need English to talk to colleagues.
> 3. I have got friends in an English-speaking country.
> 4. I like to see English films in the original.
> 5. I have got relatives in Britain or America.
> 6. I sometimes have to speak English on the phone.
> 7. I like to travel and often need to speak English.
> 8. I can speak other foreign languages.
> 9. I want to help my children with their homework.
> 10. I need to translate into English.
> 11. I plan to visit Britain or America.
> 12. I am interested in reading books and newspapers in English.

At the beginning of each unit the main language focus is stated.

Summary of functions, grammar and skills that are focused on in the Classroom section.

Important note for the teacher.

The *Procedure* section provides step-by-step suggestions on how to use the activities.

Cultural background information or language notes important for the activity.

If a file is used in the activity, a copy of it is provided in the Teacher's Book.

4 a Let the students listen and fill in as many names as possible. They can compare their completed family tree with a partner before listening for a second time to check.

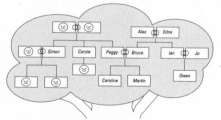

A full key is provided for all closed activities.

b Give students enough time to draw their own family tree, but start putting them into small groups as soon as they finish.

Possible answer:

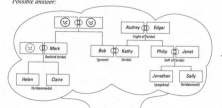

Where deemed useful, there are *possible answers* for open-ended activities. They should be treated as a guide as to what students might produce.

5 Students make a sentence individually from one of the three boxes and then find other students who have chosen different boxes and listen to their sentences.

🔑 I hope you enjoyed the class and spoke as much English as possible.
I look forward to seeing you all here again next week.
Don't forget to do your homework and prepare for the next class.

Overview of the Home study section, Teacher's Book

Each activity in the Home study section has a title indicating the topic.

Extension means that the activity goes beyond what has been done previously, i.e. new vocabulary, functions, grammar will be introduced.

If a topic has been dealt with before, a cross-reference in brackets will indicate where it came up first.

Cultural background information or language notes important for the activity.

The *VHS-Certificate* vocabulary used in the activity is listed here. Words marked with an asterisk (*) are not in the *VHS-Certificate* list, but may prove useful for the student. Words from the *Waystage* catalogue are not listed, as it is assumed that the students are familiar with this vocabulary.

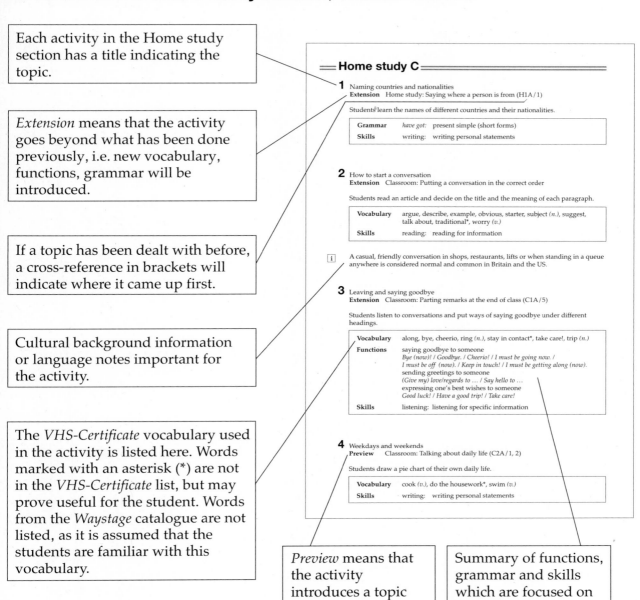

Home study C

1 Naming countries and nationalities
Extension Home study: Saying where a person is from (H1A / 1)

Students learn the names of different countries and their nationalities.

Grammar	*have got*: present simple (short forms)
Skills	writing: writing personal statements

2 How to start a conversation
Extension Classroom: Putting a conversation in the correct order

Students read an article and decide on the title and the meaning of each paragraph.

Vocabulary	argue, describe, example, obvious, starter, subject (*n.*), suggest, talk about, traditional*, worry (*v.*)
Skills	reading: reading for information

[i] A casual, friendly conversation in shops, restaurants, lifts or when standing in a queue anywhere is considered normal and common in Britain and the US.

3 Leaving and saying goodbye
Extension Classroom: Parting remarks at the end of class (C1A / 5)

Students listen to conversations and put ways of saying goodbye under different headings.

Vocabulary	along, bye, cheerio, ring (*n.*), stay in contact*, take care!, trip (*n.*)
Functions	saying goodbye to someone *Bye (now)! / Goodbye. / Cheerio! / I must be going now. / I must be off (now). / Keep in touch! / I must be getting along (now).* sending greetings to someone *(Give my) love/regards to … / Say hello to …* expressing one's best wishes to someone *Good luck! / Have a good trip! / Take care!*
Skills	listening: listening for specific information

4 Weekdays and weekends
Preview Classroom: Talking about daily life (C2A / 1, 2)

Students draw a pie chart of their own daily life.

Vocabulary	cook (*v.*), do the housework*, swim (*v.*)
Skills	writing: writing personal statements

Preview means that the activity introduces a topic before it is dealt with in class.

Summary of functions, grammar and skills which are focused on in the Home study section.

The teacher's role in pair- or groupwork

The teacher's role during these forms of interaction is very important. First of all, introduce the activity to the students and make sure that everyone knows what to do. It is always a good idea to give an example of what students are expected to do. During the activity you should move around from pair / group to pair / group, listening, helping when necessary, making (mental) notes of problems, mistakes and occasionally even taking part in the activity. After the task has been completed, round off the activity by getting pairs or groups to report on their work. You should write new words that came up during the activity on the board or OHP, so that the students have a chance to expand their vocabulary.

Finally, point out some typical errors you noticed while walking around. Ask the whole class to correct them.

Correcting mistakes

Error is a natural part of the language learning process. In some kinds of classroom activities, however, it is important to monitor the students' language and correct mistakes, otherwise the point of the activity is lost. These can be either spoken or written activities which focus on a certain grammar point, or activities which involve short writing tasks. The latter give you the opportunity to walk around and help the students to correct their mistakes. If you notice that a particular mistake is made by many students, point it out in class after the students have completed the task.

In freer, more communicative activities, especially those involving pair- or groupwork, the overall principle should be "message before accuracy". After the students have reported on their pair- or groupwork take some time to correct the most important grammar, vocabulary or pronunciation mistakes.

It has to be clear to the students that their answers to activities which focus on the learning of specific language items should be correct whereas activities which promote acquisition and fluency have the aim of producing appropriate language.

Last but not least, the students' achievements should always be measured positively, i.e. by how successfully they can use the target language for their own communicative purposes.

On Target in intensive courses

On Target is flexible enough to be used in courses with a different number of lessons available. The following suggestion provides an example of how the teaching material in *On Target* can be divided up in a six-week intensive course, for example five evenings a week with four lessons per session:

Unit 1

Monday:
Classroom / A-Block: 90 mins
Home study / A-Block: 45 mins (rest as homework)
Classroom / B-Block (first half): 45 mins

Tuesday:
Classroom / B-Block (second half): 45 mins
Home study / B-Block: 45 mins (rest as homework)
Classroom / C-Block (first half): 45 mins
Home study / C-Block: 45 mins
etc.

The Home study section done in class can be used fairly flexibly in that learners choose those tasks which best suit their individual needs. With four lessons (each lasting 45 mins) an evening learners need to be given time where they can sit quietly and work on different tasks of their choice.

Based on the above outline of an intensive teaching unit, a week will be required to work through two units of *On Target*. Within five weeks it should be possible to cover the ten units provided the learners do some work at home.

The final week could then be used for the following activities:
- work on material which so far has not been dealt with
- recycling and consolidating certain lexical or grammatical (problem) areas
- time for further activities – either the ones listed at the back of the Teacher's Book or different ones provided by the teacher.

It is feasible, however, to come up with a totally different course set up depending on the time schedule of the course. Since the latter will vary from school to school, it has to be worked out independently and adapted to the individual requirements.

We hope that you will enjoy teaching with *On Target* and wish you every success with the course.

Your *On Target* team

Unit 1 · People

Classroom A

Students learn each others' names and something about one another.

◄ ►

Functions	introducing oneself and each other; reacting to introduction *(Hello,) I'm ... / This is ... / Nice to meet you.*
Grammar	present simple *(to be)*
Skills	speaking: exchange of information about each other reading: reading sentences to decide which information is relevant listening: listening for information

☞ During the first lesson you should make sure the students understand the importance of the Home study section. It is intended to reinforce and expand material worked on in class. Draw the students' attention also to the review pages, the reading for fun and the appendix.

Procedure

1 Get the students to form groups according to the number of letters in their name. They introduce themselves to everybody in their group.

Then get them to form groups according to the number of syllables in their name and to introduce themselves or each other.
If you have a group of more than 15 students you can get them to form groups according to the initial letter of their name.

[i] In Britain and America the use of first names is common among groups working or socializing together.

2 **a** Tell the students to read the sentences in File 1, page 210, and to write down only those sentences that are true for them.

File 1 (page 210)

1. I know some of the other people in this class.
2. I need English to talk to colleagues.
3. I have got friends in an English-speaking country.
4. I like to see English films in the original.
5. I have got relatives in Britain or America.
6. I sometimes have to speak English on the phone.
7. I like to travel and often need to speak English.
8. I can speak other foreign languages.
9. I want to help my children with their homework.
10. I need to translate into English.
11. I plan to visit Britain or America.
12. I am interested in reading books and newspapers in English.

b Go round helping students as necessary and encourage them to note down new vocabulary.

c Get the students to sit in a circle for this activity.

3 Although the students may come up with other possibilities, most of them will probably group the words under status / male / female / a couple. Those who choose to categorize using word length (one syllable vs. two syllables), what applies to me vs. what does not, etc. should be considered valid contributions.

i If necessary, point out that 'cousin' can occur under 'male' and 'female'.

4 **a** Let the students listen and fill in as many names as possible. They can compare their completed family tree with a partner before listening for a second time to check.

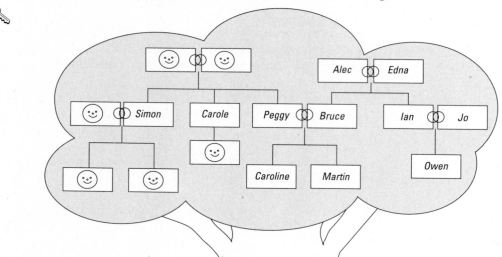

b Give students enough time to draw their own family tree, but start putting them into small groups as soon as they finish.

Possible answer:

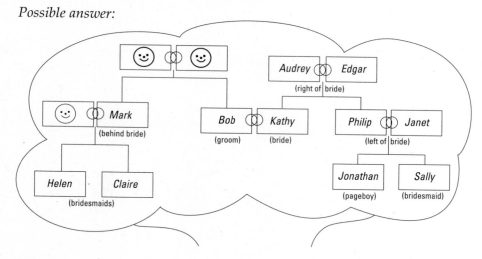

5 Students make a sentence individually from one of the three boxes and then find other students who have chosen different boxes and listen to their sentences.

I hope you enjoyed the class and spoke as much English as possible.
I look forward to seeing you all here again next week.
Don't forget to do your homework and prepare for the next class.

☞   Photocopy the alphabet game cards on page 125 for next week (B-Block, exercise1).

Home study A

1 Eliciting information about other people from various sources
Extension   Classroom: Introducing each other

Students learn to give personal information about other people and about themselves.

Vocabulary	American, birthday, born, British, children, nationality
Functions	introducing oneself *My name's … / I'm …*
Grammar	present simple (short forms) personal pronouns (subject) *have got:* present simple (short forms)
Skills	writing: note taking reading: reading for specific information

i   *Curriculum Vitae:* You write a Curriculum Vitae (CV) when you apply for a job.
It is called a resumé in American English.
Landing card: Citizens of all non-European Union countries are required to fill out a
landing card when entering Britain. Citizens of the EU need only a valid passport
or a certified state-issued identity card.

2 Giving personal information
Extension   Classroom: Noting information about other people's families and
talking about one's own family

Students learn to talk about other people's families and their own.

Vocabulary	to be retired*
Grammar	present simple (short forms) personal pronouns (subject) *have got:* present simple (short forms)
Skills	writing: writing personal statements; note taking listening: listening for specific information

3 The English alphabet
Preview   Classroom: Further practice on the English alphabet (C1B/1)

Students practise the sounds of the English alphabet.

Skills	listening: listening for specific information

i The British and Canadians pronounce the last letter of the alphabet [zed]. Americans and Australians pronounce it [zi:].

4 Greeting and introducing people formally and informally
Extension Classroom: Finding out about and introducing other students

Students listen to different ways people introduce and greet each other.

Vocabulary	hello, hi, introduce, meet, pleased, thanks *(pl.,n.)*
Functions	greeting someone; reacting to greetings *(Good) morning. / Hello! / Hi!* introducing other people *This is … / Do you know …? / Have you met …? / May I introduce …?* reacting to introductions *How do you do? (formal) / Nice to meet you. / Pleased to meet you. /* *(Hello,) I'm …* enquiring about someone's health; reacting to such enquiries *How are you? / Fine, thanks. And you?*
Skills	listening: listening for information; listening for specific information

i *How do you do?* is a common way to react when being introduced to someone you do not know very well. The correct response is *How do you do?* It is a very formal way of greeting each other, where people usually shake hands with one another.

Classroom B

Students revise spelling and dates. They will learn how to write appropriate messages on greetings cards.

◄►

Vocabulary	get married, happiness, happy, move house, wedding
Functions	expressing one's best wishes to someone *Happy birthday! / Many happy returns of the day. / Merry Christmas. /* *Happy new year. / Congratulations! / Good luck!* making suggestions *Shall we …? / Let's …*
Grammar	questions *(to be)*

Skills	speaking: focus on correct pronunciation of letters of the alphabet;
	                asking questions to elicit information;
	                making suggestions and offering personal opinion
	listening: listening for information

Procedure

1 To practise the alphabet, put the students into groups of five and give them each a card (see page 125). If you do not have the right number of students, some will have to have two cards. You say "Start" and the student who has "Start" on his/her card begins and reads **AHJ**. The student who has **AHJ** on the left side must say **LMP**, and so on. Let the students play the game twice, but they should exchange their cards after the first round.

Example:

card 1

You hear	You say
Start	A H J
EGS	XLM
ZTX	FNE
FHU	BIW

card 3

You hear	You say
AHJ	LMP
MEC	ZTX
BIW	ODH
ZEJ	Stop

2 Make sure the students understand the instructions. While they are working, walk round giving help when necessary.

Dates

Written:	Spoken:
April 2nd, 1994 April 2, 1994 Apr. 2, '94	April the second, nineteen ninety-four
2nd April(,) 1994 2 Apr. '94	the second of April, nineteen ninety-four
2.4.94	the second of the fourth, ninety-four

3 a Before doing this exercise you might want to bring in a collection of greetings cards which you look at together with the students for extra vocabulary.

a 7   b 2   c 6   d 4   e 5   f 1   g 3

Cards on all occasions (birthdays, anniversaries, graduation from college, the arrival of a new baby, a new home) are popular in Britain and in the US. 'Get well' cards and friendship cards are also popular.
It is also common to send a card or a thankyou note after being invited to an event such as a party, a brunch or a wedding. It is traditional for parents to invite guests to their children's wedding in the name of their children.

b anniversary 7; Christmas 2; new baby 1; birthday 3; wedding 6; new home 4; someone is ill 5

c Some students may need encouragement to draw, but normally enjoy the exercise once they get started.

4 Refer back to the people in 3a and, working with the whole class, collect their suggestions on the board. You could also bring a selection of pictures showing people of different ages (men and women) which students (in groups of 3–5) have to allocate to the people mentioned in 3a. Then ask students to suggest what presents they would choose for them. You can expand this activity by asking the students about presents they like or do not like to receive themselves on birthdays, at Christmas, when they move house, etc.

═ Home study B ═

1 The date and months of the year
Review   Classroom: Talking about important dates in one's own life

Students focus on dates.

Skills	reading: reading for specific information
	listening: listening for specific information

i A *born loser* is someone who can't seem to do anything right.
An ex-wife or ex-husband can also be referred to as *my ex*.

2 Ways to improve your spoken English
Extension   Classroom: Giving reasons for learning English (C1A / 2)

Students are confronted with a reading text.

Vocabulary	conversation, improve, invite s.o. over, offer *(v.)*, personnel*, practise, pub, record *(v.)*, take s.o. out, typical*, visitor
Grammar	*If* (function word) + adverbial clause
Skills	reading: reading for information

i The weather has always been a good, safe topic for starting a conversation. Maybe it is especially true in the British Isles because the weather is so changeable. The fact that it changes so often means one can hardly argue with any statement made about the weather!

3 Writing letters
Extension   Classroom: Messages on greetings cards

Students focus on various personal letters.

Vocabulary	greeting *(n.)**, invitation, note *(n.)*, parcel
Functions	beginning and ending a letter
	Dear … / Sincerely, / Love, / Yours, / Yours truly,
	sending greetings to someone
	(Give my) love/regards to …
	expressing one's best wishes to someone
	Our good wishes to you all.
Skills	writing: guided letter writing
	reading: reading for information;
	reading for specific information

▬ Classroom C ▬▬▬▬▬▬▬▬▬▬▬▬▬▬▬▬▬▬▬

Students discuss likes and dislikes and consider entertaining in different countries.

◀ ▶

Functions	expressing likes and dislikes *I like ... / I don't like ... / I prefer ...*
Grammar	present simple relative pronouns
Skills	speaking: controlled drilling of structures with students providing the context writing: note taking reading: reading for information; reading to check comprehension and construct a dialogue listening: listening for information

Procedure

1 Students should be encouraged to take ideas from the pictures. Those students who finish early could be asked to add one or two more sentences using their own ideas. Collect their papers, shuffle them and redistribute them, making sure nobody gets his/her own. When students make wrong guesses, allow the other students, along with the person who is being guessed, to comment.

2 a Students write down the two conversations in the correct order.

Dialogue 1

▲ It's very warm this winter, isn't it?

◆ It certainly is. I booked my skiing holiday six months ago and now there's no snow! Do you ski at all?

▲ Not really, no. I play a lot of tennis in the summer but I prefer to stay indoors in the winter and listen to records.

◆ Oh, I like listening to records, too. What kind of music do you prefer?

Dialogue 2

▲ The food's great, isn't it?

◆ It certainly is. I wish I could cook so well.

▲ Oh, I'm sure you can, really. What sort of things do you like cooking?

◆ Oriental food mostly. What about you?

b Encourage students to present the situation and characters of the people in the dialogue and read out their continuation of the dialogue to the rest of the class.

3 Allow the students enough time to collect their ideas individually. Then put them into groups of three or four and let them talk about what they have written.

Possible answers:
I like people who are interesting to talk to.
I like days when the sun is shining.
I like places where I can do or see something interesting.
I like teachers who are interested in what they do.
I like films which have a happy ending.
I like lessons in which I can actively participate.

I don't like people who are moody.
I don't like days when everything goes wrong.
I don't like places where there is a lot of noise.
I don't like teachers who don't prepare their lessons.
I don't like films which show a lot of violence.
I don't like lessons in which you have to sit and listen all the time.

4 a The class discussion is meant to introduce the students to the topic on the cassette which follows.

b Check the students' notes to make sure they have understood the text on the cassette. This can be done while the students are talking together about what Melanie says.

things that surprised her
everybody was sitting down; the handshaking
shaking hands
people shook hands when they arrived and again when they left
the two mistakes she made before she went to the party
she hadn't brought any flowers; she had eaten before the party
the food at the party
there was masses of food including dozens of salads
the way the Americans behaved
they just walked in and introduced themselves

c Put the students into pairs and let them discuss what Melanie says.

Extra activity

At the end of the lesson, after 4c, ask the students if they can remember any of the statements that were made by the other students during exercise 3.

Examples:
Lena likes places where she can be alone.
Martin doesn't like films which show violence.

This can be done orally or you can ask the students to write down as many statements as they can remember.

═ Home study C ═

1 Naming countries and nationalities
Extension Home study: Saying where a person is from (H1A/1)

Students learn the names of different countries and their nationalities.

Grammar	*have got:*	present simple (short forms)
Skills	writing:	writing personal statements

2 How to start a conversation
Extension Classroom: Putting a conversation in the correct order

Students read an article and decide on the title and the meaning of each paragraph.

Vocabulary	argue, describe, example, obvious, starter, subject (n.), suggest, talk about, traditional*, worry (v.)
Skills	reading: reading for information

i A casual, friendly conversation in shops, restaurants, lifts or when standing in a queue anywhere is considered normal and common in Britain and the US.

3 Leaving and saying goodbye
Extension Classroom: Parting remarks at the end of class (C1A/5)

Students listen to conversations and put ways of saying goodbye under different headings.

Vocabulary	along, bye, cheerio, ring (n.), stay in contact*, take care!, trip (n.)
Functions	saying goodbye to someone *Bye (now)! / Goodbye. / Cheerio! / I must be going now. /* *I must be off (now). / Keep in touch! / I must be getting along (now).* sending greetings to someone *(Give my) love/regards to … / Say hello to …* expressing one's best wishes to someone *Good luck! / Have a good trip! / Take care!*
Skills	listening: listening for specific information

4 Weekdays and weekends
Preview Classroom: Talking about daily life (C2A/1, 2)

Students draw a pie chart of their own daily life.

Vocabulary	cook (v.), do the housework*, swim (v.)
Skills	writing: writing personal statements

Unit 2 · Daily life

Classroom A

Students revise asking questions. They will have the possibility of working together creatively as well as finding out more about each other.

◀▶

Grammar	present simple (for things that happen repeatedly) question words
Skills	speaking: exchange of ideas and opinions in order to complete various tasks writing: guided creative writing listening: listening for specific information; listening to reinforce and check the grammar point

Procedure

1 **a** The students work individually and should be helped with vocabulary they need.

Possible answers:
Andrew and Monica live in Morton.
Their flat is **in the centre of town**.
They get up at 6.30 every morning and have breakfast.
They have **coffee, toast and marmalade.**
Andrew leaves home at 7.30. He goes to work by **bus. / He cycles to work**.
His day is often tiring but varied. He **is a bank clerk**.
Monica doesn't start work until 9.00. She **is a receptionist**.
In the evenings and at the weekends they enjoy their hobbies. Monica **sings in a choir**.
Andrew **plays football**. They both **enjoy playing cards with friends**.

b Individual papers can be read aloud and the differences in the characters they have created discussed. Students should be given a chance here to ask if sentences they have written are grammatically correct.

c Put the students into three groups A, B and C and either play the cassette or tell them you are going to read fifteen questions at normal speed. Before each question you say 'A', 'B' or 'C' and they should write down only those questions that are for their group.

A How old are Andrew and Monica?
B Where is Morton?
C What sports do they like?
A What does Andrew look like?
B What is Morton famous for?
C What hobbies have they got?
A What does Monica look like?

B What part of town do they live in?

C How much time do they spend on their hobbies?

A What are their tastes in clothes?

B What view have they got from their living room window?

C How do they spend their weekends?

A What sort of music do they enjoy?

B What are their neighbours like?

C Where do they like to go for their holidays?

d Encourage the students to work together to come up with one answer for each question.

Possible answers:

A Andrew is 35 years old. Monica is 32 years old.

B Morton is a small town in the north of Scotland.

C Andrew likes to play football and Monica likes volleyball. They often like to go hiking together as well.

A Andrew is tall, with short, dark brown hair and brown eyes.

B Morton is famous for its locally brewed Scotch whisky.

C Andrew plays football and Monica sings in a choir.

A Monica is also tall, with fairly short, blonde hair and green eyes.

B They live in a flat in the centre of town.

C Every weekend, Andrew spends Saturday afternoons playing football and Monica spends Sunday mornings singing in a choir.

A They both like to wear casual but smart clothes.

B From their living room window they can see the main shopping street in Morton and in the distance the hills which lie to the west of the town.

C Apart from spending time on their hobbies, Andrew and Monica often go shopping together on Saturday mornings at the big supermarket just outside of town. They also like to meet people from the football club in the local pub on Saturday nights and often play cards with friends on Sunday evenings.

A Andrew likes rock music and Monica likes classical and pop music.

B Their neighbours are a friendly, retired couple.

C They like to go somewhere where it is hot and sunny and where they can swim in the sea. Last year they went to Greece.

e Regroup the students, ideally in groups of three, with one student from A, B and C, so that they can exchange their information. Using the answers they have produced in 1d, they write a description of Andrew and Monica and their daily life. This can be done either on an OHP transparency or on a piece of paper that can be circulated for everyone to read.

2 **a** Let the students listen to the cassette all the way through before they start to fill in the correct questions. Go round individually checking the questions. Get them to ask others to help with any information they did not manage to get after the first listening. The students should listen to the dialogue again to check their answers.

1. When do they get up?
2. Does Amy get a bottle, too?
3. What do they have for breakfast?
4. What do they like for lunch?
5. Does Chris usually sleep in the afternoon?
6. Do they have a bath before bed?
7. Does Amy know where things are?

b The students are given further practice in asking questions and have the opportunity to personalize.

3 Put the students into pairs or groups of three. Point out that for some words it may only be possible to give a definition or a translation, whereas other words can be explained more easily by a drawing.

Possible answers:

tiring:	working long hours every day can be very …
neighbours:	the people who live next door to you
famous:	another word for *well-known*
information:	a tourist guide gives you … about the town you are visiting
instructions:	you need to read these before, for example, you use your new video recorder
remember:	when you think of a word you had forgotten, you … it
friend:	someone you trust and can turn to when you have a problem
varied:	vielfältig
usually:	gewöhnlich
taste:	Geschmack, schmecken
worried:	besorgt
dirty:	schmutzig

juice:

breakfast:

bottle:

Home study A

1 The time
Review   Classroom: Saying what time people do things

Students review how to ask for and tell the time.

Functions	addressing someone
	Excuse me, …?
	making requests
	Could you …? / Do you know …? / Have you got …?
Skills	listening: listening for specific information

2 A quiz: Are you a morning or a night person?
Review   Classroom: Talking about daily routine

Students answer questions about their own habits as well as those of another person.

Vocabulary	midday*, complete (v.), depend, enjoy, have breakfast, healthy, last (n.), really, rise (v.), wealthy*, wise
Grammar	present simple (do questions) short answers (with do/don't) frequency adverbs: position
Skills	writing: writing personal statements reading: reading for information listening: listening for specific information; listening and responding

i When talking about a time between 0.00 and 12.00 noon *a.m.* (ante meridiem) is used after the hour if there is the possibility that it may be unclear what time is meant (2 a.m.). For the times between 12 noon and midnight *p.m.* (post meridiem) is used for the same reason (2 p.m.). The 24-hour clock is used for flight timetables and increasingly rail and other timetables. Times in this system are read as normal digital times, the full hours being read ... hundred hours.

13.20   *thirteen twenty*
17.07   *seventeen oh seven*
18.00   *eighteen hundred hours*

For further information on the time of day look at page 237 in the grammar section.

3 A letter to the babysitter
Review   Classroom: Telephone conversation about children's daily routine

Students complete a note from information they have heard in class (C2A/2a).

Vocabulary	brush one's teeth*, fridge*, hall, neighbour, potato salad, pretty, swim (v.)
Grammar	present simple (3rd person singular)

Classroom B

Students look at the daily life of each other and of other people through listening and reading.

◄►

Grammar	present simple (3rd person singular)

Skills	writing: factual statements about students' daily life;
	                guided creative writing
	reading: reading students' texts to check content;
	                skimming a difficult text for information;
	                reading to find omitted vocabulary
	listening: listening for information to complete a written task

Procedure

1 Make sure the students really understand the instructions. If necessary, give a full example by writing five sentences on the board and the students then have to guess your lie. Stress that the lie should be hard to identify.

Example:
I play tennis every Tuesday.
I teach fourteen lessons a week.
I have a cup of coffee in the afternoon.
I do the washing and ironing twice a week.
I do a lot of shopping every Friday morning.

2 Get the students to take notes while they are listening to the dialogue. After you have gone over the completed charts let them listen to the cassette again.

6.45:	alarm rings
6.50 to about 7.30:	gets up / gets dressed / wakes the children / has breakfast
7.40:	takes the children to school
just after 8.00 to 12.00:	gets back home / has coffee / reads the newspaper / wakes her husband / makes the beds / tidies up / goes shopping / has coffee / does the cleaning / does the washing
just after 12.00:	collects the children from school
12.30:	gets lunch
after lunch:	does the dishes

Ask individual students to compare their routines with Peggy's.

3 **a** Look at the picture of Madeleine Brain with the students and ask general questions about her appearance, age, life style, etc.

b Let the students individually answer the eight questions in note form. From the notes they should write a coherent text. Go round helping with vocabulary where necessary.

c As soon as the students finish get them to exchange papers to read while the slower students still continue writing their text.

d Silent individual reading. The students should read the text quickly.

e In pairs students try to predict the missing words. Students who find the task difficult can look at File 3, page 210, which will help them find the missing words.

File 3 (page 210)

check	give	pay
cook	go	say
cope with	goes	spend
deal with	have *(2x)*	starts
do	keep *(2x)*	stay
eat	love	take over
ends	manage	talks
enjoy	meet	tidy up
find	open	wakes

1. wakes	11. manage	21. go
2. do	12. meet	22. have
3. keep	13. eat	23. cook
4. open	14. keep	24. love
5. check	15. give	25. enjoy
6. deal with	16. starts	26. spend
7. pay	17. talks	27. stay
8. cope with	18. take over	28. say
9. goes	19. ends	29. find
10. have	20. tidy up	

f The students compare their own texts from 3b with the original one in 3d.

Home study B

1 Daily routine at home
Extension Classroom: Listening to the first part of an interview with Peggy talking about her daily routine

Students listen to the rest of the interview with Peggy and complete a chart.

Vocabulary	dish (n.), fix (v.), gymnastics*, lesson, look after s.o., plant (n.)*, take care of s.o.
Grammar	present simple (for things that happen repeatedly)
Skills	writing: note making listening: listening for specific information

2 A song about a couple who reversed roles
Extension Classroom: Talking about daily routine

Students listen to the song *Turning it around*, put pictures in the correct order and find definitions for new vocabulary.

Vocabulary	block (n., v.), bored (adj.), business, consider*, excitement, firm (n.), fool (n.), fun, go crazy*, happy, kid*, laugh (v.), laundry*, lawyer, nervous strain*, normal, ordinary, pioneer*, proud, stupid, test (n.), useful, worried (adj.)
Functions	expressing feelings *Did he feel worried/proud of himself? / Does he feel happy and useful?*
Skills	reading: reading for specific information listening: listening to check answers; listening for enjoyment

The word *ditch* (*Turning it around*, line 7) means *to get rid of, discard*. *To ditch someone* is a slang expression.

Ain't is a contraction of *am/is/are not*. It is used in non-standard spoken English. Although it is disapproved of in written English, *ain't* is used orally in some parts of Britain and many parts of the United States. It is more common in less educated speech. It is also used at all education levels to deliberately draw attention both in speech and in writing. Last but not least, it is used in pop songs for metrical reasons.

Bar exam: An exam that law students have to take in order to be qualified to practise law.

3 Jobs and places where people work
Preview   Classroom: Talking about jobs and places to work (C2C/2, 3)

Students preview vocabulary they will need for the next lesson by unscrambling words and matching pictures to different jobs.

> **Vocabulary**   computer programmer, cook *(n.)*, flight attendant, hotel manager, mechanic*, lifeguard, pilot *(n.)**, secretary, shop assistant, waiter

> [i]   You might want to point out that, in English, many professions and jobs refer to both men and women doing the job. There are a few exceptions, i.e. *waiter/waitress, actor/ actress, businessman/businesswoman, chairman/chairwoman*. One should note here that non-sexist terms have been entering the language since the seventies. *Server* is sometimes used in American English for *waiter* and *waitress*. Words such as *chairperson* are also common. *Person* is used as a suffix to avoid *man* in compound words that apply to both sexes.

▬ Classroom C ▬

Students discuss likes and dislikes in connection with work. They learn new vocabulary in the context of jobs and professions.

◄ ►

Functions	expressing likes and dislikes
	I like ..., but I don't like ... / I'd like ... / I'd prefer ...
	giving reasons
	I like / I don't like ... because ...
	maintaining a conversation
	What does ... mean?
Grammar	present simple (negation)
Skills	speaking: controlled drill;
	defining and paraphrasing vocabulary
	writing: note making;
	writing statements using information from texts
	reading: reading for detail

Procedure

1 Make sure the students can see and hear each other if it is not possible to sit them in a circle. Let everybody make a statement and then get them to try to remember what was said.

2 **a** Help with vocabulary if necessary but only after the students have had the opportunity to help each other.

1. *Duty/Activity:*   cares for the sick
2. *Job:*   lawyer
3. *Duty/Activity:*   makes and repairs wooden things
4. *Place:*   sorting office and out in the street
5. *Job:*   waiter / waitress
6. *Duty/Activity:*   buys and sells houses
7. *Place:*   plane
8. *Duty/Activity:*   sells goods, advises customers
9. *Place:*   garage

The job of an *estate agent* in Britain is to find buyers for houses, land or other property which is up for sale.

b After the students have made notes, get them to call out their ideas, which you should then record on the board under [+] and [−].

c Make sure the students know the meaning of the listed words before they set out to do the task. With a weak class you may have to give examples yourself first.

d Allocate about ten minutes for this activity and let the pairs work at their own speed talking about as many of the jobs as they have time for.

Possible answers:

nurse: responsibility, recognition in society, contact with other people, team work, physically active, job security, challenge

postman/-woman: decent environment, contact with other people, physically active, job security

flight attendant: variety, responsibility, contact with other people, team work, job security, challenge, good salary

shop assistant: decent environment, contact with other people, part-time, challenge

3 **a** The students should read the texts silently and ask you individually if they have problems with the vocabulary.

Jerry Linngren
Julie Taming

A *business lawyer* is a lawyer who is employed by a company to deal with all their legal matters.

b The students have to read the texts from 3a again and be able to extract the relevant information to write statements.

Possible answers:
Ted: I like my job because I learn something new every day.
Sandy: I like my job because I can work on my own.
Bill: I like my job because I have a lot of freedom.
Jerry: I don't like my job because I see things that could be done better, but I can't change anything.
Harry: I like my job because I like to be active.
Julie: I don't like my job because I do the same things every day.

c As this is intended as a free-talking activity, concentrate on the content rather than on any errors that may occur. Draw the students' attention to the structure given in the speech bubble: *I'd like … because …*

Extra activity

Write jobs (e.g. policeman/-woman, baker, tourist guide, aerobics instructor, taxi driver, artist, factory worker, etc.) on sticky labels which you attach to the back of each student. They have to walk around asking *yes/no* questions in order to guess their job. You might want to suggest appropriate questions before they begin and write them on the board.

Examples:
Do I work outdoors?
Do I earn a good salary?
Have I got a lot of responsibility?
Do I produce something?

Home study C

1 Talking about work routine
Extension Classroom: Talking about likes and dislikes at work

Students listen to a quiz show and try to guess what jobs the people on the show have.

Vocabulary	early/late shift*, full-time, indoors*, next door*, outdoors*, part-time, passenger, public holiday, ride one's bike, serve, shiftwork*, take the bus, travel benefit*, uniform*, walk (v.), wear (v.), view (n.)
Grammar	present simple frequency adverbs: position
Skills	writing: writing personal statements listening: listening for information; listening for specific information; listening and responding

2 Living and working in Europe
Extension Classroom: Talking about work and home (C2A, B)

Students read a text about the lives of three different European families.

Vocabulary	afford, clerk, collect, earn, fishing, freezer*, gadget*, home computer, insurance company, leisure*, monthly cost, overtime*, pay (n.), pocket money, spend, two-bedroomed flat, typist, washing machine
Skills	writing: guided note taking reading: reading for information; reading for specific information

Unit 3 · Places

Classroom A

Students work with a map to identify places and revise prepositions that are needed in this context. After using the map from Great Britain they will have the possibility of speaking about their own area.

◄ ►

Functions	asking for and giving information *Where's the bus stop? It's near the supermarket.*
Grammar	prepositions questions
Skills	speaking: controlled dialogues using the prepositions presented in the listening text listening: focusing on specific information from a dialogue

Procedure

1 **a** Ask the students to identify the pictures and then brainstorm other places one would expect to find in a small town (e.g. supermarket, park, police station, school, cinema, restaurants, etc.).

bus stop	4
pub	6
church	5
station	2
newsagent's	3
statue	1

b In pairs let the students have a closer look at the map of Gravesend and complete the sentences with the prepositions given in the box.

1. opposite
2. on the corner of
3. next to, in

Gravesend is a small town and river port on the right bank of the River Thames, downstream from London. Early settlement in the area can be traced back to about 2,000,000 years ago and many great figures in English history passed through Gravesend on their way to the capital. The town grew considerably in the 19th century and Gravesend's present day industrial significance is closely tied to transport on the Thames and involves paper mills, ship repairing and engineering industries.

c The students listen to the first part of the dialogue and complete the sentences individually with the prepositions given in 1b.

1. on the corner of
2. next to
3. in
4. in
5. opposite

d The students listen to the second part of the dialogue and complete the sentences with the prepositions given. The activity can be expanded by asking the students to describe places in their area, e.g. *The church is opposite the market. The car park is behind the school.* This will be preparation for the following exercise.

1. on the left, on the right
2. between
3. behind, near
4. in front of

2 **a** The students tick the places they pass on the way to class. They can add other things that are not listed.

b In pairs the students should be encouraged to use the prepositions practised in the previous activities.

3 **a** This activity is meant as revision of known vocabulary. In groups the students have 25 slips of paper. They write a word on each one. As soon as the groups finish, get them to shuffle the words and exchange their pile with another group. The groups now sort out the words they have been given under the headings provided. They then ask the group who wrote the words if the categorization was as they had intended.

Possible answer:

STATUE	HOTEL	CAR PARK	TELEPHONE BOX	MARKET
large	modern	central	dirty	busy
stone	elegant	expensive	useful	colourful
impressive	big	pay and display	coin-operated	noisy
famous	new	multi-storey	international	fruit
beautiful	well-known	large	broken	interesting

b Each group can join up with another group and the 50 words can be sorted out under FACT and OPINION.

Possible answer:

FACT	OPINION
large	beautiful
new	elegant
central, etc.	interesting, etc.

Home study A

1 Talking about a country place: West Clare County in Ireland
Extension   Classroom: Talking about a town

Students learn to talk about what you can do in West Clare County and focus on descriptive vocabulary.

Vocabulary	area, bird-watching, caravan park*, cycle*, fish (v.), horse-riding, lighthouse, local, man-made, natural, play golf*, pollution-free*, quiet, swim (v.), tourist information, traditional*, typical*, unusual*, view (n.), walk (v.), wild flower, wind-surf*
Grammar	*there + be* modal verb: *can* (possibility)
Skills	writing: note making reading: reading for specific information

i

Fens and bogs: An area of low, very wet land is referred to as fen or the fens. A wet muddy area is called a bog. These areas are also called marshes, swamps or wetlands.

West Clare County: It is situated on the west coast of Ireland. For more information on Ireland write to:

Irische Fremdenverkehrszentrale
Untermainanlage 7
60329 Frankfurt am Main

You might want to get your students to write a letter in English requesting information in English.

2 Asking and explaining where things are
Extension   Classroom: Saying where things are

Students look back at the map of Gravesend (page 52) and answer questions about the town.

Functions	asking for and giving information *Is there a …? / Where's the …? / It's … / Yes, there's one … / No, there isn't, but there's … / I'm sorry, I don't know.*
Grammar	questions *there + be* (questions) *one*
Skills	listening: listening and responding

3 Asking the way
Extension Classroom: Asking and giving directions

Students listen to the dialogue C3A1c/d again and practise different ways of asking for directions.

| Functions | addressing someone
Excuse me, ...
asking for information
Can you tell me the way to ...? / Where's the (nearest) ...? / Is there a ...? |
|---|---|
| Grammar | questions |
| Skills | listening: listening for specific information;
listening and repeating |

Classroom B

Students continue to practise giving instructions to find a place on a map and talk to each other about routes.

| Functions | giving information
Turn left/right into ... Street. / Go down ... / Go straight on till you come to ... / Cross ... / When you get to ... |
|---|---|
| Grammar | imperatives
present simple (questions) |
| Skills | speaking: planning a route;
controlled practice of question forms;
partner dictation
listening: focus on listening to each other and reacting in a spoken or written form to information heard |

Procedure

1 a Before the students decide where they would like to live, they discuss the different areas of the town and the type of houses they would find there. For further information on different types of houses see page 93.

b In a large class you might want to put students into two groups.

c This exercise could be expanded to get the students to talk about where they really live and plan a route.

d Get the students to match the signs (1–8) to the words (a–h) in the box and decide where they might be found on the map.

  a 5   b 2   c 6   d 1   e 7   f 3   g 8   h 4

e The students describe to each other the route they take home from class. They can work in pairs if they wish. They then find a new partner and retell precisely the route they heard from their previous partner.

2 **a** Make sure the students do not show each other where they enter the names in their block of flats.

Ground floor vs. first floor: In British English, the *ground floor* of a building is the floor that is level with the ground outside. The *first floor* of a building is the floor immediately above the ground floor.
In American English, the *first floor* of a building is the floor which is level with the ground outside.

b Go over the instructions for this activity, explaining that the principle is similar to "Battleships" *(Schiffe versenken)*. You can limit the students to only asking six questions.

3 Student A looks at File 4 (page 210) and student B at File 10 (page 212). Make sure that the students know they should not look at each others' file. The students should write their text on a separate sheet of paper, leaving enough space to fill in the missing parts of the sentences.
Student A then begins by dictating the first part of the sentence and student B fills in the missing words in his/her text. Student B then continues in this way until each student has the complete text. Make sure that the students dictate the full punctuation (commas, full stops) to each other.

File 4 (page 210)

Student A
A young man tells his friend how to get to his flat.
"When you leave … cross the road … . On the left … the Park Hotel, … in front of it. … on the left … . Church Street is … on the right. … on the corner and … is opposite the newsagent's. … the second floor, … . I don't think … finding it."

File 10 (page 212)

Student B
A young man tells his friend how to get to his flat.
"… the station … and go straight ahead. … you will soon see …, which has a large car park … . Take the first road… after the hotel. … the second road … . There is a post office … Number 6 … . I live on …, flat D. … you will have any problem … ."

A young man tells his friend how to get to his flat.
"When you leave the station cross the road and go straight ahead. On the left you will soon see the Park Hotel, which has a large car park in front of it. Take the first road on the left after the hotel. Church Street is the second road on the right. There is a post office on the corner and Number 6 is opposite the newsagent's. I live on the second floor, flat D. I don't think you will have any problem finding it."

Home study B

1 Following directions
Extension   Classroom: Giving directions

Students listen to a dialogue and follow the directions to find a certain spot on the map of Keswick, a tourist town in the Lake District.

Vocabulary	along, look out for, main road, nature trail*, uphill*
Functions	asking for and giving information
Can you tell me the way to …? / Do you know where … is? /
How do I get to …? / Certainly, go up there and turn right.
Grammar	prepositions
Skills	listening: listening for specific information

i | *Keswick* is a market town in the northern part of the Lake District National Park in Cumbria. It lies at the north end of the lake known as Derwent Water. Keswick is a scenic tourist resort which attracts thousands of visitors every year. Lead mining was formerly of economic importance here. In Victorian times Keswick was well-loved by poets and artists, including such notables as Wordsworth, Coleridge, Southey, Ruskin and Walpole. Many of their works and personal possessions are preserved in the fascinating Fitz Park Museum.

2 Asking the way / giving directions
Extension   Classroom: Asking for and giving information (C3A1/2; C3B/1)

Students review asking the way and following directions.

Vocabulary	path*, youth hostel*
Functions	asking for and giving information
Can you tell me the way to …? / Do you know where … is? /
How do I get to …? / Go down … / Turn left/right into … /
Keep straight on …
Grammar	questions
imperatives
prepositions
Skills	reading: reading for specific information
listening: listening for specific information;
listening and responding

3 Talking about different countries
Extension Classroom/Home study: Talking about towns and country areas (C+H3A)

Students read the information given and decide which country is being described.

Vocabulary	average, capital *(n.)*, Christian, coal, dairy product*, descent*, forest, gold, language, major export*, natural gas, natural resource*, population*, religion, separated from, silver *(n.)*, wool
Functions	asking for information *What is/are …? / Where is …? / How much …?*
Grammar	question words
Skills	reading: reading for specific information

i The facts about New Zealand and Ireland were taken from *The Almanac 1993*, a valuable source for looking up all kinds of facts and information.

4 Crosswords
Review Classroom: Describing a town

Students focus on adjectives by filling in the opposites of the words used to describe cities and the countryside.

Vocabulary	(un)attractive, boring, dirty, exciting, (un)interesting, noisy, (un)polluted*, pretty, quiet, ugly

Classroom C

Students are given information about Nottingham. They write about a place they know well and plan a trip for visitors around their own town.

Functions	making suggestions *You can …*
Grammar	adjectives present simple modal verb: *can* (ability, possibility)
Skills	speaking: discussing a task that involves coming to a concensus in the group writing: writing a short descriptive text reading: reading for information

Procedure

1 **a** Collect words and ideas on the board (a kind of brainstorming).

b This should be a silent reading activity.

Sport	2
Entertainment	1
Famous people	3
Shopping	5
Museums and historic buildings	4

c This is a comprehension exercise. After the students finish they can compare and supplement their lists with a partner.

You can go to a night club/restaurant/pub.
You can go to the disco/cinema.
You can go swimming.
You can play badminton/table tennis/squash.
You can have a sauna/Turkish bath.

d As 1c.

There are a lot of night clubs/discos/cinemas/theatres/restaurants/pubs/historic buildings/shops.

e You can make suggestions here, e.g. *a place where you spent a holiday, the place where you grew up, a place where you enjoy yourself,* etc. Students should have a chance to ask for words, or to have their texts corrected after the task has been completed.

2 With classes of less than twelve students leave out some of the visitors so that each group consists of at least two students. Go round helping as needed and encourage the students to make an original, interesting programme. A speaker from each group should go to the front of the class and present the programme.

Possible answer:
At 9.00 a.m. we will meet the Brazilian engineering student at her hotel. We will go by underground to the old town where we can look at the interesting buildings, the river and the cathedral. If she is interested, we can go up the cathedral tower to the observation platform to get a good view of the city. If it is raining, we will go to the museum to see the exhibition of models of the town. After an early lunch at a pleasant restaurant overlooking the river, we will take a taxi to a factory where they make lifts. We have made an appointment with the chief engineer for 2.00 p.m. and he will give us a guided tour of the factory. At about 4.30 p.m. we plan to have a cup of tea or coffee before going shopping with our guest. She will probably want to return to her hotel for an hour or so before we meet to go to dinner in a restaurant of her choice.

3 **a** The students work individually.

🔑
small / tiny
old / ancient
interesting / fascinating
valuable / priceless
big / huge
good / excellent
useful / invaluable

b The students can either work individually or in pairs. If time is short, exercise 3b can be done on the board with the whole group.

🔑

VALUE	QUALITY	SIZE	AGE
priceless	good	small	old
valuable	excellent	tiny	ancient
useful	interesting	big	
invaluable	fascinating	huge	

Home study C

1 Los Angeles: A personal view
Extension Classroom: Talking about a city, what it is like and what you can do there

Students read a personal description of LA. They write down the advantages and disadvantages of the city and do a crossword puzzle which reviews vocabulary from the text.

Vocabulary	advantage, civil disorder*, culture*, decide, earthquake*, exotic*, fascinating*, fault (n.), flood (n.), move (v.), order (v.), public transportation*, relaxing*, sense of humour
Functions	expressing likes and dislikes *She likes … / It was love at first sight. / … has two qualities I value …*
Grammar	present simple
Skills	reading: reading for information; reading for specific information

ℹ️ *Smog:* This word is a combination of the two words *fog* and *smoke.*

Venice Beach is a suburb just north of the Los Angeles International Airport. Town planners conceived the town to be a new world copy of the historic city it was named after, but it never lived up to its name. Nowadays it is a rather shabby town that attracts young people. Malibu, Newport Beach and Laguna Beach are the more stylish beach resorts. Venice is the capital of the "laid-back" Californian beach bum life style. Many people meet to enjoy sun-bathing, swimming, beach volleyball, basketball, street music, cycling, roller-blading or skating, or just looking at the action.

2 Describing a town or country area
Review   Classroom: Talking about towns (C3A, B)

Students review vocabulary by describing places mentioned in the unit so far.

Vocabulary	crowded, industrial, medium-sized*, place (n.), residential*, resort*, tourist
Grammar	prepositions

3 Living in different places
Extension   Classroom: Talking about towns (C3A, B)

Students listen to an interview with two Englishmen talking about the places they were born, where they grew up and where they live now.

Vocabulary	bare*, cultural centre*, dull, grow up, mountainside, plenty, remote*, suburb	
Grammar	past simple	
Skills	writing:	note taking
	listening:	listening for information;
		listening for specific information;
		listening and responding

Unit 4 · Food

Classroom A

Students are given new vocabulary in the area of food and work on dialogues in the context of shopping.

Functions	offering help *What can I do for you? / Can I get you anything? / Anything else? /* *Can I help you?* asking for things *Have you got any …? / How much would you like? / How many? / What sort?* saying what you want *I'd like some …*
Grammar	modal verb: *would* (polite way of saying what you want) *much/many* *some/any*
Skills	speaking: constructing new dialogues using previously written models writing: controlled production of dialogues listening: extracting specific information from a dialogue; checking predicted dialogues

Procedure

1 **a** Go round helping students individually with difficult vocabulary.

tin of mushroom soup	23
jar of marmalade	8
jar of strawberry jam	12
packet of tea	15
salt	4
sugar	3
flour (1 kilo)	26
a large chicken	13
2 lamb chops	24

Cheddar cheese (1/2 lb.)	10
2 bottles of orange juice	9
1/2 doz. cans of coke	22
2 bottles of red wine	2
onions (2 lb.)	16
tomatoes (1 lb.)	14
potatoes (5 lb.)	6
1/2 doz. rolls	1
loaf of brown bread	7

mince (1 lb.)	25
ham (1/4 lb.)	27
oranges (10)	17
apples (1 lb.)	19
butter (1/2 lb.)	20
doz. eggs	11
2 pints of milk	5
cream (1/2 pt.)	21
ice cream	18

b The students should listen to the cassette before they fill in the list. They will probably need to listen at least once more before they can complete the task. The students should copy the table before they start filling things in.

Item	How much?	How many?	What sort?
soup	a tin		mushroom
marmalade	a jar		the cheapest
tea	a packet		Typhoo
sugar	a kilo		
eggs		a dozen	large
cream	half a pint		
cheese	half a pound		Cheddar
orange juice		two bottles	
coke		half a dozen cans	
tomatoes		a pound	Spanish
rolls		half a dozen	
bread	a loaf		large, brown

i | *Marmalade vs. jam: Marmalade* is a type of jam made from the pulp and peel of oranges, or other citrus fruit, and is usually eaten for breakfast. *Jam* is made from all other fruit.

In American English jam is called *jelly*.

2 Encourage the students to stand during this activity and, as soon as they have finished, to walk around and find a new partner.

3 a While the students are filling in the missing sentences, go round correcting any errors.

b The students will probably only need to listen to the cassette once before they practise the dialogues with a partner.

c Change the students around so that they are now working with a new partner. They should be encouraged to construct the dialogue without notes using phrases practised in 3a and 3b. Pairs who finish quickly can swap roles and work on a new dialogue while waiting for the slower students.

Extra activity

Get the students individually to make a list of ten things they like to eat and ten things they do not like to eat. You may have to help students with vocabulary while they are writing their lists. Write on the board *I like that, too. / I don't like that either.* When the students read out their lists, get other students to comment using the two structures mentioned above.

Home study A

1 Food Guide Pyramid
Extension   Classroom: Food vocabulary

Students review food vocabulary by writing a list of the foods they have eaten that day and comparing it with the healthy foods recommended in the Food Guide Pyramid.

Vocabulary	bean*, fat (*n.*), meat, nut, oil (*n.*), pork, poultry*, serving (*n.*), snack, sweet (*n.*), yoghurt
Grammar	modal verb: *should* (advice)
Skills	writing: note making reading: reading for specific information

i

Yoghurt: This word has various spellings which may cause confusion. *Yoghurt* is also spelled *yoghourt* or *yogurt* in British English. *Yogurt* and *yoghurt* are both used in American English. In the exercises we have used British English spelling (yoghurt) and in the original American texts the American English (yogurt).

The Food Guide Pyramid was developed by the US Department of Agriculture in order to help people learn to eat healthy foods. It can be found on many products.

2 Shopping for food
Review   Classroom: Shopping for food

Students review asking for things in shops by listening to the cassette and writing short dialogues.

Functions	asking for things and saying what you want *Have you got any …? / I'd like some … / Two kilos, please.*
Grammar	*some/any* *much/many* modal verb: *would* (polite request)
Skills	listening: listening for specific information

3 Reading the menu
Extension   Classroom: Food vocabulary

Students study the London Park Hotel menu and become familiar with new vocabulary by answering questions and finding the odd one out.

Vocabulary	alcohol-free, apple sauce*, beverage*, cabbage*, carrot*, cereal*, chip*, custard*, ham*, lemonade*, mashed potato*, pasta*, pea*, pie*, plaice*, prawn cocktail*, roast beef, VAT (value added tax)*
Skills	reading: reading for specific information

i

Yorkshire Pudding is not a dessert. It is a light, puffy, savoury baked dish made from a batter of flour, eggs and milk, traditionally served with roast beef.
The word *pudding* is also used to mean dessert.
Custard is the name of the sweet, vanilla-flavoured sauce that the British pour on fruit pie and other desserts.

Types of British beer
Ale: Beer made in the British way, which is different from the way in which lager, for example, is made. It is brewed from barley, which has been malted (i.e. softened in water and allowed to germinate). Traditional British ale has no gas in it and it is not served very cold, which enhances the taste. Real ale (draught beer) is sold in the traditional pub.

Bitter: The most popular kind of British beer. It has a high hop content and tastes slightly bitter. It can be keg (i.e. a method, which uses a gas called carbon dioxide) or traditional draught (i.e. it has no gas in it, and a pump is used to draw the beer up the pipe and out of the tap).

Guinness: A thick, almost black, bitter-tasting Irish beer.

Lager: A light beer, served cold, that is common in many countries. It is matured over a long period of time at a low temperature.

Bottled beers: There are several kinds available, e.g.:
light ale (like pale ale, i.e. less strong and a bit sweeter than bitter)
brown ale (a brown often rather sweet beer)
stout (a very dark beer, produced from the brewing of roasted malt)

Asking for beer
In Britain beer is sold in pint glasses (570ml) and half pint glasses (285ml). You will need to say how much beer you want and what kind, e.g.:

| A | pint half | of | bitter, lager, | please. |

Classroom B

Students practise ordering meals in a restaurant and learn new vocabulary to describe food and services.

◀▶

Functions	saying what you want *I'll have … / I'd like (some) … / I'll try … / We'd like …*
Grammar	modal verbs: *will* (when we decide to do s.th. at the time of speaking) *would* (polite way of saying what you want) past simple (*to be*)

Skills	speaking: talking about meals and personal experience in the
	                    context of restaurants;
	                    creative role play
	listening: intensive listening to dialogues which provide a model

Procedure

1 The completion exercises to the listening 1a–e should be done individually. Check after each stage and if necessary play the cassette a second time.

a Jon: We'd like a table for two, please.
   Sue: Can we have the wine list, please?
b Sue: soup, roast beef, Australian wine
   Jon: fruit juice, grilled lamb, pint of bitter
c Jon: **I'll have** grilled lamb.
   Sue: **I'd like** roast beef. / **I'll try** the Australian wine.
d the bill, coffee, apple pie, fruit
e Waiter: Did you enjoy your meal?
   Jon: Yes, it was excellent.
   Sue: The roast beef was delicious.

2 **a** Collect information from the whole class getting students to explain any of the dishes that are unfamiliar to the others.

[i]

Tacos: savoury dish made from maize flour eaten in Mexico.
Fried rice: a dish made from a combination of meat, vegetables and rice eaten in China.
Paella: fish, chicken and saffron-flavoured rice from Spain.
Poppadums: savoury accompaniment to curry, popular in India.
Risotto: a rice dish from Italy.
Spring rolls: Chinese pancakes filled with meat and vegetables.
Moussaka: minced lamb and aubergines eaten in Turkey and Greece.
Bortsch: a soup made from beetroot, eaten in Russia.

tacos – Mexican; fried rice – Chinese; paella – Spanish; poppadums – Indian; risotto – Italian; spring rolls – Chinese; moussaka – Turkish/Greek; bortsch – Russian

b In a very small class this could be done as class discussion with students talking about their experience in different restaurants. With more than ten students, however, group work seems to be more efficient.

3 **a** Go round helping students with vocabulary. Get them to write a menu which includes different courses, beverages and also the prices. Make sure the dishes are appropriate to the restaurant they have chosen.

b Encourage the students to use phrases practised in the previous exercises. They should tell the pair ordering a meal what sort of restaurant it is. They may even want to add whether it is an expensive, high-class, cheap or fast-food restaurant.

4 **a** Get the students to write their lists and then compare with a partner.

Positive: excellent, delicious, very tasty, nice and dry, fresh, dry (e.g. wine), cold (e.g. beer), tender

Negative: burnt, salty, too sweet, tough, stale, dry (e.g. rolls), cold (e.g. coffee)

b If time is short, they do not have to do all the words, but can choose foods from the box that they want to work on.

Possible answers:
Chicken: excellent, delicious, very tasty, burnt, tough, cold, tender, dry
Omelette: excellent, delicious, very tasty, burnt, salty, cold
Soup: excellent, delicious, very tasty, salty, cold
Wine: excellent, delicious, nice and dry, too sweet, dry, cold
Rolls: delicious, burnt, stale, dry, fresh
Pork chops: excellent, delicious, very tasty, burnt, tough, dry, cold, tender
Fish: excellent, delicious, very tasty, burnt, salty, fresh, dry, cold
Fruit salad: excellent, delicious, very tasty, too sweet, fresh, cold
Steak: excellent, delicious, very tasty, burnt, tough, dry, cold, tender

Home study B

1 Breakfast in the US
Extension Classroom: Eating out in a restaurant

Students read a text on going out for breakfast in the USA and note the differences in customs.

Vocabulary	cashier's desk*, custom, host/hostess*, include, motel*, serve, tip *(n.)*, waiter/waitress
Skills	reading: reading for information; reading for specific information

Smoking in restaurants: More and more cities around the US are banning smoking completely in all restaurants within the city limits because it is better for business. It seems there are more people who would rather go out to a smoke-free restaurant than there are people who want to smoke.

2 Understanding the menu and ordering breakfast
Extension   Classroom: Ordering a meal in a restaurant

Students focus on vocabulary used when ordering breakfast in a restaurant or coffee shop.

Vocabulary	bacon*, cinnamon roll*, doughnut*, melon*, omelette*, pancake*, pastry*, plain *(adj.)*, sausage, strawberry*
Functions	asking for information *Would you like …? / How many, please? / Can I get you anything else?* maintaining a conversation *Can you tell me what … is/are? / It's a … / They're …*

Skills	reading: reading for specific information
	listening: listening for specific information;
	                listening to check answers;
	                listening and responding

i

Eggs in the US: When you order eggs in the US the server (non-sexist term for waiter/waitress) will always ask you how you want your eggs. Possible answers are: sunny-side-up (fried with the yolk unbroken), scrambled, easy-over (a well-done sunny-side-up egg), shipwrecked (an egg fried on both sides), soft/hard boiled.

In America, a *muffin* is a small cake. There are corn muffins and blueberry muffins. In Britain, a *muffin* is a thick, round cake which can be served toasted and spread with butter.

▬ Classroom C ▬

Students discuss food and health. They share opinions before reading an article on the topic. Finally, they work on word associations related to the topic of food.

◀▶

Functions	warning *Beware of …! / Look out …! / Mind …! / Danger! / Take care!*
Skills	speaking: sharing opinions about food and health; discussing and explaining word associations writing: note taking in order to produce a coherent text reading: reading a newspaper article for global understanding

Procedure

1 a Give each student a number and tell them to find their question in File 12 (page 213). They should then copy the table from the Student's Book (page 84) and write down the question with the number. Students then ask as many people as possible in the class their question. Get them to write down the names of all the students they ask and note brief answers to the question. If you have more than fourteen students either add questions to the following list or use some of them twice.

File 12 (page 213)

> 1. What do you think about diets?
> 2. What do you think about smoking?
> 3. What things don't you like to eat?
> 4. What do you do to try to stay fit and healthy?
> 5. What is your idea of a healthy breakfast?
> 6. Do you eat certain meals on certain days?
> 7. What do you think about vegetarianism?
> 8. Where and when do you eat your main meal of the day?
> 9. What vegetables do you like to eat and how do you cook them?
> 10. Do you eat differently from ten years ago?
> 11. What do you like to cook when you invite friends to your home?
> 12. What do you drink in the evening?
> 13. Do you ever eat fast food and do you think it is harmful?
> 14. If you go out to eat, what sort of meals do you enjoy?

b Ask the students to write their names at the top of a piece of paper. Collect the papers and distribute them taking care that nobody gets his/her own name. Tell the students to talk to others in order to collect as much information as possible about the person whose name they have received. They are not allowed to talk to the person directly, but must ask other students what their question was and how it was answered.

c Give the students enough time to order the information and prepare a short profile of the person whose name they have been given. They should write in the present simple and not be allowed to use indirect speech. In classes with more than ten students the number of students presenting their profile to the rest of the class should be kept to a minimum.

2 2a and 2b can be done individually, but 2c is probably more fun when done with a partner.

   a 1. B   2. A   3. E   4. F   5. C   6. D
   b A 1, 5   B 3   C 2, 4
   c *More popular:* salads, fruit, vegetables, vegetable oil, low-fat milk, chicken, fish, soft drinks, sweeteners, cereals, rice, wine, low-calorie beer
     Less popular: bacon, butter, red meat, white sugar
     Not mentioned: sausages, yoghurt, eggs, whisky

3 It will be necessary to work out a couple of examples on the board to show the students the range of different possibilities and let them see that there is no correct answer. The students work individually, but compare their vocabulary with other students as soon as they finish.

The following numbers *three*, *seven* and *nine* have been chosen as examples to demonstrate the various possibilities of completing the task.

Possible answers:

3.

7.

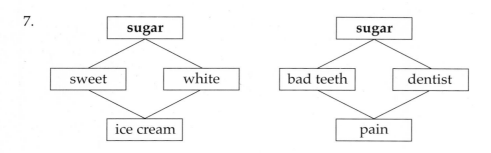

9.

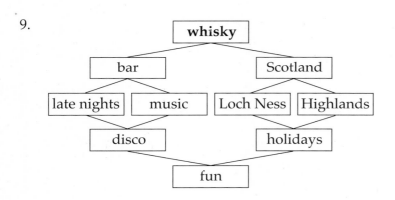

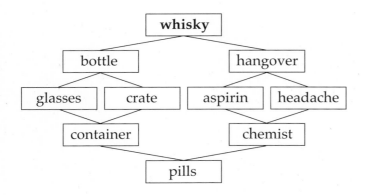

i *New-age travellers* are people who are not settled in one place. They move in large groups with their caravans around the countryside and often come into conflict with the rural communities where they make their camps.

═ **Home study C** ═

1 The Yogurt Mill Restaurant
Extension   Classroom: Talking about healthy eating habits

Students listen to an interview with the manager of a health food restaurant and look at the menu.

Vocabulary	chocolate, district, flavour*, frozen yoghurt*, healthy, popular
Skills	reading: reading for specific information listening: listening for information; listening for specific information

i
Most Americans eat their main meal (dinner) in the evening when they come home from work. People either take their lunch to work or go out for a light lunch or snack around noon. Children can eat a hot lunch at the school cafeteria or take their own lunch. Sandwiches made out of peanut butter and jam or bananas are especially popular.

2 Changing your habits
Extension   Classroom: Talking about healthy eating habits

Students read a newspaper columnist's comment and practise giving advice.

Vocabulary	cause (*v.*), dangerous, disease*, nervous, recommend, work out
Functions	giving advice and advising against *I would (not) … if I were you. / You really ought to … / I recommend you …*
Grammar	modal verbs: *ought to* (moral obligation) *would* (advice, *if*-clause) present perfect simple
Skills	reading: reading for information; reading for specific information listening: listening to responses

i
Newspaper columnists are very popular in the US. Most large newspapers carry at least 15 columns each day. The columnists comment and give their personal opinions on political issues, events, social issues, news stories, trends, the use of the English language, personal problems or just modern life in a humorous way in order to get their point across.

Booze is a slang expression for alcohol.

3 Food for thought
Review   Classroom: Food vocabulary review

Students focus on vocabulary by grouping foods from the menus into categories.

Skills	reading: reading for specific information

Unit 5 · Services

Classroom A

Students focus on the bank and the post office and talk about the services offered. They will have a chance to reactivate passive vocabulary by practising known words in new situations.

◀ ▶

Functions	making requests *May I ...? / I'd like to ... / Would you ...?*
Grammar	present perfect simple modal verb: *can* (possibility)
Skills	speaking: discussing and justifying word association and classification; role play using previously practised models listening: recognizing specific information

Procedure

1 a The students should work in pairs and then present their word roses on the board or OHP.

Possible answer:

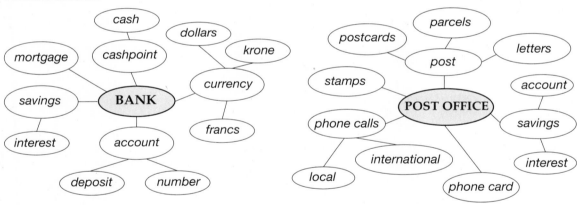

b Discuss the pictures with the whole class and get the students to note down the ideas that come up. Help them with the vocabulary.

Possible answers:

Similarities:	Differences:
There is a counter in both photos. There is a person to serve you. Glass screens separate the clerk from the customer.	There is a cash dispenser at the bank. There are weighing machines at the post office. There are more counters at the bank than at the post office.

c Lead the discussion over to services at the bank and post office. You might want to divide the class so that one group is working on the bank and the other on the post office. They can then exchange papers and supplement each other's lists.

Possible answers:
Bank: You can transfer money. You can get foreign currency. You can take out
                a loan. You can invest money. You can cash a cheque.
Post office: You can buy stamps. You can send a parcel. You can open a savings account.
                You can send a registered letter.

i   In Britain and the US you do not collect your new telephone directory from the post office – it is delivered to your door. It is also not normally possible to make a phone call at the post office.

d   Write the following chart on the board. Collect students' ideas in the middle of the chart, as in the example.

How many things have you done during the last two weeks?

* ——————————————————————————————— *

2 weeks ago   today

> I've bought some stamps.
> I've sent letters.
> I've used the cashpoint.

Further possible answers:
Bank: I've collected my statement. I've paid my bills. I've ordered new cheques.
                I've discussed investment. I've transferred money to my savings account.
Post office: I've bought postcards. I've collected a registered letter. I've sent a telex.
                I've sent a greetings telegram.

2   **a**   Let the students listen once and tick the boxes. They compare their solution with a partner and then listen again.

At the post office: 1, 2, 4
At the bank: 2, 4

b   Get the students to sequence the dialogue and to practise it with a partner. Those students who finish quickly can swap roles and practise the dialogue a second time.

A   Good morning, can I help you?
B   I'd like to cash a traveller's cheque.
A   May I see your passport, please?
B   Here you are.
A   Would you fill in your name and address in the United Kingdom
     and sign here, please?
B   Yes, certainly.
A   That's fine. How would you like your money?
B   It doesn't matter, but I'd like a pound in small change, please.
A   20, 30, 35, 36, 37, 38, 39.50 and five 10p pieces makes £40.
B   Thank you, goodbye.
A   Goodbye.

c Student A looks at File 8 (page 212) and student B at File 17 (page 214). Pairs that finish early can be told to switch roles.

File 8 (page 212)

Situation 1: You are a tourist in Britain and go to the post office to send five postcards and a letter home. You don't know how much the letter costs. You have no small change. You would like to know how long letters take.

Situation 2: You are a clerk in a bank in Britain.

File 17 (page 214)

Situation 1: You are a clerk in a post office.

Situation 2: You are a tourist in Britain and go to the bank to cash a Eurocheque. You are not sure of the rate of exchange or of the maximum amount you can cash per cheque. You would also like to know how much the bank charges are for each cheque you cash.

3 **a** Stress that the students should try to define the word they have chosen without using it and the others have to guess it. An alternative is for you to write the words from 3a on strips of paper and give one to each student.

i A *cashpoint* is a machine on the outside of some banks where you can take out money at any time by using a special card *(cashpoint card)* and typing in your personal number.

An *operator* is a person who deals with phone calls, telecommunication services and any problems which arise. In some cases it is not always possible to dial certain countries direct, so you ask the operator to get the number you want. Operator calls, however, are more expensive.

b Put the students into pairs or small groups. There are several ways of classifying the vocabulary and their suggestions can be discussed in the whole group.

Possible classifications:
Bank / Post office / both Bank and Post office / Phoning / Post / Money

Home study A

1 Asking for things at the post office
Review Classroom: What you can get at the bank and at the post office

Students practise writing questions and listening to how much things cost.

Functions	making requests *I'd like ...*
Grammar	questions (*Can ...? / How much is ...?*) modal verb: *would* (polite way of saying what you want)
Skills	listening: listening for specific information; listening to check answers

2 Clothing
Preview Home study: Shopping for clothes (H5A/3)

Students become familiar with words used to describe clothing by labelling pictures and deciding what to take on a trip.

Vocabulary	accessory*, boot (*n.*)*, cardigan*, cotton, footwear*, glove*, handbag*, material, sandal*, suit (*n.*), tie (*n.*), tights*, trousers*
Skills	writing: labelling

3 Shopping for clothes
Extension Classroom: Shopping for food (C4A/2, 3)

Students listen to and practise language used in clothes shops.

Vocabulary	dressing room*, exchange (*v.*), fit (*v.*), jacket, pullover, receipt, shorts, style*
Functions	making requests *I'd like to … / Can I …?*
Grammar	comparison of adjectives
Skills	listening: listening for information; listening for specific information; listening and responding

4 A quiz: Are you the adventurous type?
Extension Classroom: Talking about what you have done during the last two weeks (C5A/1d)

Students answer questions about different experiences they have had.

Vocabulary	adventurous, alone, discover, fly (*v.*), outside, recently, star (*n.*), swim (*v.*)
Grammar	present perfect simple
Skills	reading: reading for information; reading for enjoyment

Classroom B

Students practise useful phrases for telephoning in English. They will share information about their shopping habits with others in the class.

◄ ►

Grammar	infinitive with *to* (expressing the decision to do s.th.) frequency adverbs

Skills	speaking: speculation on suitable dialogues for a given situation;
	                 oral drill to practise frequency adverbs and idiomatic phrases
	writing: constructing dialogues from notes provided
	listening: listening to provide students with a model;
	                 listening to check completed dialogues

Procedure

1 **a** The students work individually, but will probably need to hear the dialogue twice. You can then recall the actual language used in the dialogues.

b The students work in pairs and should note down the appropriate language from the telephone chart.

(answers also on the cassette)
◆ Hello?
▲ Hello, this is Pat. Can I speak to Katrin?
◆ Just a moment. I'll get her.
● Hello?
▲ Hello Katrin, it's Pat.

c As 1b. After listening to the cassette, the students discuss differences between their dialogues and the recorded ones.

(answers also on the cassette)
◆ Hello?
▲ Hello, this is Pat. Could I speak to Carol, please?
◆ I'm afraid she's out. Shall I give her a message?
▲ That's very kind of you. Can you tell her I'll be arriving at 8.30.
◆ Sorry, could you repeat that, please?
▲ At 8.30.
◆ OK. I've got that.
▲ Thank you very much. Goodbye.
◆ Bye.

2 a Draw the following grid on the board and fill in appropriate questions as suggested by the students.

Possible answers:

① Do you have any passport application forms?

② Do you open on Saturdays?

③ How many different sorts of bread do you have?

④ Good morning. I'd like some first class stamps, please.

⑤ Is it possible to have breakfast served at 6 a.m.?

⑥ Do you have any rooms free?

⑦ What time do you close for lunch?

⑧ Could I make an appointment to see the manager tomorrow?

⑨ Shall I put the shoes back on the shelf?

Bank	Post office	Shop	Hotel	Museum	Answers
	①				Over there by the window.
②					I'm afraid not.
		③			Fifteen.
	④				Yes, certainly.
			⑤		I'll just check that for you.
			⑥		Not at the moment.
				⑦	From 12 to 2.30.
⑧					Yes, I'm sure that would be possible.
		⑨			That's very kind of you.

b This activity can be done individually or with the whole class.

Possible answers:

Customer: I need to renew my passport. Do you have any passport application forms?
Clerk: Over there by the window. Just take one and fill it in.

Customer: Excuse me. I've heard some banks are open at weekends now. Do you open on Saturdays?
Clerk: I'm afraid not. We're only open Monday to Friday.

Customer: My goodness! What a lovely selection of cakes, breads and pastries you have here. How many different sorts of bread do you have?
Baker: Fifteen. We bake all our own bread using recipes from all over the country.

Customer: Good morning. I'd like some first class stamps, please.
Clerk: Yes, certainly. How many would you like?

Guest:	I have to make an early start tomorrow. Is it possible to have breakfast served at 6 a.m.?
Receptionist:	I'll just check that for you …Yes, that's fine. I'll have it brought to your room, if you like.

Guest:	Good afternoon. Do you have any rooms free?
Receptionist:	Not at the moment. I'm afraid there's a big conference in town this week so we're fully booked.

Visitor:	Excuse me. What time do you close for lunch?
Curator:	From 12 to 2.30. Here's a leaflet with some more information. You'll find our opening hours on the back page.

Customer:	Good morning. I'm interested in taking out a loan. Could I make an appointment to see the manager tomorrow?
Clerk:	Yes, I'm sure that would be possible. What time would suit you best?

Customer:	Oh, dear. I'm afraid these are too big for me. Shall I put the shoes back on the shelf?
Shop assistant:	That's very kind of you. It will save me doing it! Shall I get you a smaller pair?

3 **a** Before students set out to complete the task, the three photos could serve as a means of recycling vocabulary. The class can be split up into three groups with each group looking at one picture only and making a list of things (preferably on an OHP transparency) that can be obtained from their particular shop. Each group then presents their list which can be supplemented by the rest of the class.
Individually the students then match items from box A and B by drawing lines across.

You go to a **chemist's** to **get some medicine**.
You go to a **record shop** to **look for CDs**.
You go to a **dry cleaner's** to **get your coat cleaned**.
You go to a **baker's** to **buy rolls and a cake**.
You go to a **jeweller's** to **get your watch repaired**.
You go to a **butcher's** to **buy sausages and meat**.
You go to a **bank** to **use the cashpoint**.
You go to a **kiosk** to **get a newspaper**.
You go to a **florist's** to **buy a bunch of flowers**.
You go to a **greengrocer's** to **buy vegetables**.

i	A *chemist's* in Britain is a shop where you can get medicine on prescription. You can also buy health foods, other medicines, cosmetics and some household goods.

b The emphasis on this exercise is to practise frequency adverbs such as *never, seldom, hardly ever, now and again, a couple of times a week,* etc.

Ask students to bring a tool or gadget to the next lesson (C-Block, exercise 3). It should be something unusual, so that the others have to guess what it is used for. You should try and bring some unusual gadgets in yourself which can be used alongside the students' objects.

≡ Home study B ≡

1 Making a phone call
Extension Classroom: Talking on the phone

Students focus on telephoning. They listen to two people discussing how to phone Germany.

Vocabulary	area code*, dial *(v.)*, fault, worry *(v.)*
Functions	apologizing and reacting *Sorry about that. My fault. / That's OK. Doesn't matter. / Don't worry.* asking for help and reacting *Do you know how to …? / Yes, I think so. First you …*
Skills	reading: reading for information listening: listening for specific information

2 Talking on the telephone
Extension Classroom: Talking on the telephone

Students listen to telephone conversations and focus on introducing themselves on the phone and asking for someone.

Vocabulary	message, repeat, ring up
Functions	talking on the telephone *Hello, this is … / My name's … / Hello, … here. / Hello, it's … / Is that …? /* *… speaking. / I'll put you through. / I'm afraid she's out. / I'm afraid he's* *not in. / OK. I've got that.* making requests *Could I …, please? / Can I …? / I'd like to … / Could you repeat that, please?* expressing thanks and reacting *Thank you very much. / That's very kind of you. / Not at all.* offering to help *Sure, … I'll get her. / Shall I give her a message?* apologizing *I'm very sorry … / Oh, I'm sorry.*

Grammar	modal verbs: *could* (polite request)
	              can (request)
	              shall (offer or suggestion)

Skills	listening: listening for information; listening for specific information

Classroom C

Students talk about their experience of buying and selling second-hand goods and read about a garage sale.

Functions	giving advice	
	Be sure you … / It's a good idea to … / We recommend you … / We suggest you …	
	asking and explaining the purpose of something	
	I wonder what this could be? / What's this for? / It's a … / It's used for …	
Grammar	present perfect	
	modal verb: *could* (polite request)	
Skills	speaking:	talking about personal experiences when buying and selling; finding out about unusual objects by asking questions or speculating
	writing:	writing a drill by using information from the text to reinforce the grammar point
	reading:	reading to find information and to identify speech functions
	listening:	listening to reinforce the grammar point

Procedure

1 Get the students to walk around collecting information from each other. Make sure the students use the present perfect question *Have you ever …?* Allow the activity to continue as long as the students are interested in each other's experiences. The purpose of this activity is to bring the students together again into groups and share any interesting experiences.

2 a The students read the article silently and fill in the boxes, which they can then check by working with a partner.

1. 1, 2, 6, 7
2. 10, 11, 12, 13

People in the US often have a *garage sale* to get rid of old, unwanted items which they no longer use. Garage sales are often held on the driveway of a house. The items for sale are priced and arranged on tables or on the ground. People then come and have a look around, buying anything they like.

In Britain *car boot sales* are often held in empty car parks or on school playing fields. People drive to the sale and park their cars with the boots open and then arrange the items for sale either on a table near the boot or actually in the boot of the car. The items are priced and people can walk from car to car, buying what they fancy.

b Before the students start listening to the conversation, put the following questions on the board.

What has Susan already done?
What has Gene already done?
What does Susan need to do?
What does Gene need to do?

After the first listening students tick the correct answers in their coursebook. After the second listening collect the answers about what Susan and Gene have done. Finally, students concentrate on the things that still need to be done by Susan and Gene.

Susan: She's made a list. She's put price tags on everything. She's been to the bank. She's painted her old table and chairs.

Gene: He's put price tags on everything. He's made the posters. He's washed the glasses.

Susan: She needs to make a cash box. She needs to clean out the garage. She needs to wash some dishes.

Gene: He needs to make a list. He needs to put up the posters. He needs to paint the baby bed. He needs to look through old books.

c This exercise should be done in pairs or small groups.

1. Be sure	6. It's a good idea to
2. Be sure	7. We recommend you
3. Be sure	8. We recommend you
4. It's a good idea to	9. We suggest you
5. It's a good idea to	10. We suggest you

3 Collect the objects students have brought to class and add one or two things you have brought in yourself. Put the students into small groups so that each group gets two or three gadgets. They discuss the use of the objects and then present them to the whole class. If they have been unable to decide what the object is, they should invent a use. When it is presented the owner can comment.

Home study C

1 What's it for?

Extension Classroom: Asking what things are used for (C5C/3)

Students practise asking about unusual objects and describing what they are used for.

Vocabulary	bake*, bowl (*n.*)*, candleholder*, decoration*, doll*, maybe*, measure (*v.*)*, medicine, old-fashioned*, peanut butter*, pepper*, salt, spice*, towel, wall, wonder (*v.*)
Functions	expressing uncertainty *It could be … / It might be … / It may be … / Perhaps, … / Maybe it's for …* asking and explaining the purpose of something *What do you think this is? / What's this for?/ I wonder what this could be?/ It's used for … / You can use it for … / I think it's a …*
Grammar	modal verbs: *could* (supposition) *may/might* (possibility)
Skills	reading: reading for information listening: listening for specific information

2 Sunday shopping: Arguments for and against
Extension   Classroom: Talking about where you buy certain things (C5B/3)

Students read an article on shopkeepers' opinions on the subject of Sunday opening.

Vocabulary	believe, during, employ, employee, florist, hairdresser, jeweller*, optician*, overtime, owner, shopkeeper*, staff (*n.*)*, travel agent*
Functions	stating an opinion *I'm all for it. / I think it's … / I believe … would be a good thing. /* *I'm (not) in favour of … / I'm absolutely against it. / I'm opposed to … /* *It seems to me that … / I'm dead against it.*
Grammar	*If*-clause (hypothetical condition)
Skills	writing: personal statements reading: reading for specific information

Shop-opening hours in Britain: Opening and closing times vary according to the type of shop as well as to the area of a city or town. The usual opening time for shops is from 9.00 to 17.00, 17.30 or 18.00 from Monday to Saturday. Many shops are also open on Sundays.

General stores have different opening and closing times, though some have the same hours as shops. They are usually open from 7.00 to 18.00 or 21.00, seven days a week.

Supermarkets open from 9.00 till 18.00 Mondays till Saturdays; many open till later (e.g. 20.00). In big cities, for example in London, there are so-called midnight stores that stay open for 24 hours.

Off-licences usually stay open from 8.30 to 23.00 Mondays to Saturdays and on Sundays 12.00 to 14.00 and 19.00 to 22.30.

In busy shopping and tourist areas shops do not close at lunchtime. In different areas of cities and towns, there is often one day of the week when shops are open for evening shopping *(late night shopping)*, i.e. till 20.00 or sometimes even later, and one afternoon a week when some shops are closed *(half day closing)*.

Unit 6 · Holidays

Classroom A

Students discuss likes and dislikes in connection with holidays and speculate about those of other people.

◄ ►

Functions	expressing likes and dislikes *I like … / I love … / I want … / I am interested in … / I enjoy … / I prefer …*
Grammar	present simple (+ noun phrase, gerund or infinitive)
Skills	speaking: explaining and justifying opinions and ideas writing: writing sentences to reinforce the grammar point reading: reading to collect information to use in different contexts

Procedure

1 **a** Give the students enough time to read and mark their preferences and write down any other things they can think of.

b Encourage the students to leave their seats, to show each other what they have marked and give their reasons.

2 Ask the students to skim the holiday adverts and when they have made a decision tell the rest of the class which person they have chosen and which holiday. If some students have chosen the same person but different holidays a discussion may develop.

Possible answers:

First person: Barbados would be a good choice. It is hot and sunny – you could stay at Buccaneer Bay for two or three weeks.

Second person: The tour of Albania would be ideal for you. You can travel around and visit lots of fascinating places.

Third person: A Sunsites camping or caravanning holiday would be great for all the family. It is self-catering, so you can cook your own meals.

Fourth person: Get away from it all on a peaceful cruise ship – you can do as much or as little as you like!

3 **a** Help the students with vocabulary if they need it.

b Get the students to write the holiday they suggest on their partner's paper. You can help weaker students individually by starting them off with phrases like:
I suggest you … / I think you should … / … would be a good choice.

c You might want to expand this into a class activity where the most popular, least popular, etc. holidays are discussed.

4 Put the students into small groups. Give them time to think and maybe make a few notes. With a small number of students you could have a class discussion.

☞ If you are planning to do the extra activity on page 67 in the next lesson, tell the students to bring in a photo of themselves taken on holiday.

Home study A

1 Choosing a holiday
Extension   Classroom: Talking about what you like and dislike on holiday

Students listen to a couple discussing different holidays and focus on suggestions and reacting to suggestions.

Vocabulary	brochure, crowded, joke (v.), reasonable, self-catering*, serious, tiring
Functions	making suggestions and accepting/rejecting *How about …? / If you like, we can … / Let's … / Shall we …? /* *We can/could (always) … / What about …? / Why don't we …? /* *You must be joking! / I'd quite like to, but … / I'm sure that's very reasonable,* *but … / Sounds good. / That's a good idea. / Right, let's do that!*

Grammar	modal verbs: *can/could* (suggestion)
	                       must (logical conclusion)
	                       shall (offer or suggestion)
	adjectives

Skills	listening: listening for specific information

2 Don't forget!
Extension   Classroom: Holiday vocabulary

Students look for words in a wordsearch puzzle and review holiday vocabulary.

Vocabulary	camera, forget, guidebook, map (n.), phrase book*, swimming costume*
Skills	reading: reading for specific information

i	BE	AE
	swimming costume	bathing suit
	driving licence	driver's license

3 Booking a room
Extension   Classroom: Asking for information (C4A/2; H3A/2, 3)

Students practise getting a hotel room, making a reservation on the phone and writing a letter to reserve a room in a hotel.

Vocabulary	arrival, inn*, harbour (n.)*, landlady, landlord*, main lounge*, view (n.)
Functions	asking for information *Have you got …?/ Is there a … in the room? / What time is …?* beginning and ending a letter *Dear Madam,/Sir, / Yours sincerely,*
Skills	writing: writing a letter listening: listening for information; listening for specific information

▬ Classroom B ▬

Students talk about past holidays and exchange their experience with others in the group.

◀ ▶

Grammar	past simple (statements and questions using regular and irregular verbs)
Skills	speaking: answering and asking questions; presenting a summary of information; dictating sentences; asking for more information about events in the past
	writing: writing dictated sentences
	reading: reading to reinforce past tense irregular verbs
	listening: listening for information to answer specific questions

Procedure

1 **a** Get the students to listen with closed books and then discuss with the whole class which question Bruce and Peggy are answering.

What was your worst holiday?

b Tell the students to read the questions before the second listening. After they have filled in the table they can compare answers with a partner and a third listening may be needed to check any discrepancies.

1. *Peggy:* Wales / her family / by car / four days / tent / don't know / rained all the time / no
2. *Bruce:* Italy / the school / by train / don't know / hotel / didn't enjoy it / very hot / no

2 **a** Tell the students to write their questions on a sheet of paper where they can also note down answers they hear. Allow enough time for the interviewing.

b Encourage every student to report back at least one thing. In a small class (less than eight students) write everybody's name together with the information they give on the board.

3 The students work in pairs. Student A looks at File 5 on page 211. Student B looks at File 9 on page 212. As each pair finishes the puzzle they can check their answers with other pairs.

File 5 (page 211)

> **Student A**
> 1. The Allens flew to California for a month where it was very hot.
> 2. The family who stayed in a hotel did not like the food.
> 3. The family who took the car on a camping holiday was lucky and had very good weather.
> 4. The family who went to Britain for three weeks did their own cooking, so they thought the food was wonderful.

File 9 (page 212)

Student B
5. The family who took a short trip to the Alps for a week's walking were very disappointed as it rained every day.
6. The family who spent most of the holiday visiting friends found that the food varied: sometimes it was wonderful, sometimes it was terrible. They had nice rooms to stay in.
7. The Bakers, who travelled by train, had the shortest holiday.
8. The Cooks wanted to travel around.

Allens: California / flew / a month / visit friends / nice rooms / varied / very hot
Bakers: the Alps / by train / a week / go walking / hotel / didn't like it / rained every day
Cooks: Britain / by car / three weeks / travel around / camping / wonderful / very good

4 Tell the students to read the list and only mark the statements that are true for them. In pairs, allow them to talk about their holidays for as long as they wish. Go round correcting any errors in the past tense question form. Pairs who finish very quickly could be put into new pairs to explain and expand on their statements with a new partner.

Paella is a Spanish dish made from saffron-flavoured rice with chicken and seafood.

Extra activity

Students have brought in holiday snaps. Get them to put each photo together with a blank sheet of paper on the table. Ask them to walk around looking at the photos. They should write questions they would like to ask about the photos on the sheets of paper.

Examples:
Was it always very hot?
Did you swim every day?
Did you manage to climb to the top of that mountain?

Each student then takes his/her photo and the accompanying sheet of paper and answers any questions in class that have been written.

Home study B

1 Talking about your holidays
Review Classroom: Bruce and Peggy talk about their childhood holidays.

Students listen to the cassette again and fill in the past tense forms.

Vocabulary	awful, complain, decide, fed up with*, move (v.), offer (v.), pack (v.), rise (v.), sick (adj.), tent, storm (n.), trip (n.)
Grammar	past simple (regular and irregular verbs)
Skills	listening: listening for specific information

2 A terrible holiday!
Extension Classroom: Talking about holidays

Students identify things in a picture and write sentences about what went wrong on someone's holiday.

Vocabulary	airline, balcony, cloud (n.), criminal, discussion, mirror (n.), queue (n.), reception desk, swimming trunks*, umbrella, upset (adj.)
Grammar	past simple (regular and irregular verbs)
Skills	reading: reading for information

3 Visiting the Lake District
Extension Classroom: Saying what you have done in the last two weeks (C5A/1)

Students listen to a dialogue and focus on the contrast between what people have or have not done.

Vocabulary	actually, fantastic*, find, scenery, shine (v.), spend, though (adv.)
Grammar	past simple (regular and irregular verbs) present perfect simple (negative sentences, questions and short answers)
Skills	reading: reading for information listening: listening for specific information

i   *The Lake District* is a popular tourist area in the northwest of England. Keswick lies in the centre of the Lake District, Windermere lies in the south. The Lake District is famous for its splendid lakes, beautiful mountains and lovely views. Hiking and water sports are popular in this area.

4 Our holidays
Review Classroom: Holiday puzzle

Students look back at the puzzle they worked on in class and write two short letters about the Bakers' and the Cooks' holidays.

Vocabulary	all in all, disappointed, terrible, wonderful
Grammar	past simple (regular and irregular verbs, questions)
Skills	writing: writing a letter

▬ Classroom C ▬

Students read a holiday anecdote for enjoyment and co-operate to create holiday stories themselves.

◄►

Grammar	past simple (statements, questions)	
Skills	writing:	guided composition through questions and answers to construct a complete text
	reading:	reading for enjoyment

Procedure

1 **a** As students read silently help them with vocabulary, but only after you have encouraged them to guess the meaning from the context. They should also complete the task individually.

Amsterdam 3   Cologne 4   Bonn 5   London 1   Brighton 2   Rüdesheim 6

A *budget tour* is a cheap way of travelling. It is a complete package which includes transportation (normally by coach), accommodation and guided tours.

b Encourage the students to scan the text looking for the information they need to complete the task. They work with a partner.

1. ⊟   2. ⊞   3. ⊞   4. ⊟   5. ⊟   6. ⊟   7. ⊞   8. ⊟

c In pairs only one student should write the statements.

1c   2a   3d   4h   5b   6i   7f   8g

2 **a** In a large class (more than 12 students) subdivide the groups. Insist that the groups write at least 15 questions – more if possible – since the later ones are often more interesting and imaginative. Allow enough time and suggest to the "secretary" of each group that space is left on the sheet for answers to be added. The students read the questions they receive and invent answers which are then written on the question sheet.

Possible answers:

Group A   They went to Denmark.

When did they go?	Last August.
How did they travel?	By car.
Where did they stay?	In a rented summer house.
How long did they stay?	Four weeks.
Where was their accommodation?	On the coast.
What was it like?	Large and well-furnished, but not very clean.
Etc.	

b The students use the questions and answers they get from the other groups to write a text. Ideally, this is done on an OHP transparency to facilitate reading. If an OHP is not available, either photocopy the texts or make a wall display. Errors or improvements can be dealt with as a class activity.

Possible answer:
Last August we travelled to Denmark by car. We stayed for four weeks in a large and well-furnished summer house at the coast. Unfortunately, the house was not very clean, etc.

═ Home study C ═

1 What's that?
Extension Home study: Expressing uncertainty about something (H5C/1)

Students look at pictures of San Francisco and guess where they were taken.

Functions	expressing certainty and uncertainty *That's … / That must be … / That's probably … / That looks like … /* *That might be … / I've got no idea what that is.*
Grammar	modal verbs: *might* (possibility) *must* (logical conclusion)
Skills	writing: writing sentences

i

San Francisco is said to be one of the world's most beautiful cities because of its fabulous geography. It is surrounded on three sides by water so the bracing smell of the sea is everywhere. Panoramic views can be enjoyed from the famous viewpoints such as Twin Peaks or Nob Hill.

The weather, which is said to be a perpetual fall climate, is also unique. To be sure, there is a good deal of rain, and there is the thick, regular fog. But the more frequent, local type of fog is an important ingredient of the San Francisco atmosphere. In low-hanging drifts it roams around the bay and between the hills, hiding parts of the town in a white blanket while other areas are crystal clear.

Not only is San Francisco's location fascinating but also its multi-cultural history. Chinatown is the largest Chinese settlement outside Asia, and the oriental influence is found everywhere throughout the city. The names of many famous places attest to the European influence in the city and today there are still ethnic neighbourhoods where a native can feel like a foreign tourist.

2 A walking tour of San Francisco
Extension Classroom: Giving advice (C5C/2; H6A/1)

Students listen to a dialogue which includes suggestions for a walking tour of San Francisco and take notes on what you can do or see in certain areas.

Vocabulary	craftsman*, foggy, fountain*, natural history museum, sunset
Functions	giving advice and reacting *If I were you, I'd … / You should … / You might want to … / If you like …,* *there are … / I can recommend … / If …, you should … / Maybe I'll … /* *I'll remember that. / That sounds like a good idea. / I will. /* *Sounds interesting/nice. / Good, let's go there.*
Grammar	*If*-clause (hypothetical condition) modal verbs: *might* (possibility) *should* (advice) *will* (promise)
Skills	writing: writing personal statements listening: listening for specific information

i

In American English the city centre is called *downtown*.

3 Holiday crossword
Review   Classroom / Home study: Holiday vocabulary

Students review vocabulary by completing a crossword.

Skills	reading:	reading for information; reading for enjoyment

Unit 7 · Travel

Classroom A

Students are introduced to the topic of transport and discuss forms of transport they use. They read an article on travelling around the US by bus.

Functions	making suggestions
	you can … / you may have to … / it's a good idea to … / it is best to … / why don't you … / what about …
	comparing things
	… is slower than … / … is more expensive than … / … isn't as good as …
Grammar	comparison of adjectives
Skills	speaking: talking about forms of transport; controlled oral drill to reinforce the grammar point; making suggestions for tourists getting around
	reading: reading to recognize the author's intention to inform, give advice and make suggestions
	listening: listening to recognize vocabulary items

Procedure

1 **a** Start by asking the students which forms of transport they regularly use, occasionally use, or never use. Find out how they feel about the various forms of transport. In pairs students match the sentences (1–10) to the words (a–g) in the box. They then talk to other students about what they have written. There may be differences of opinion to discuss.

1. "It doesn't cost much."	a, g
2. "It doesn't run often enough."	b, e, f
3. "It's far too expensive."	b, c, d, e, f
4. "It's healthy exercise."	a, g
5. "It's OK when the weather's nice."	a, g
6. "It's too far to the nearest stop."	b, e, f
7. "It takes too long."	a, g
8. "Parking is a problem."	c
9. "They pollute the environment."	b, c, d
10. "You can never get a seat."	b, e, f

b This can be done in small groups or with the whole class.

Possible answers:
I usually walk to work because the office is only 1km away from my flat.
I usually cycle to class if the weather is nice. But if it's raining I drive.
There are shops quite close to where I live, so I usually walk. But I get the bus back if I have a lot of shopping to carry.
I fly to my hometown in Spain to visit my family.
I take the tube from home to the nearest airport because it's usually difficult to find a parking space.
I always take the tram to my favourite restaurant which is on the outskirts of town.

i Encourage the students to use *I walk* rather than "I go on foot".

c With a good class ask students to complete the sentences before listening to the cassette. Another alternative would be to play the cassette with the books closed and get the students to note down the different forms of transport they hear from memory.

"I usually go to work **by bike**, but if it's raining heavily **I walk**."
"We sold our last **car** about ten years ago."
"For longer trips we usually travel **by train**."
"And when we go to England in the summer we always **fly**. If you haven't got a car you can afford to **take a taxi** occasionally, as well."

d Get the students to look carefully at the sketch before they listen to the cassette. Individually they complete the information before listening again to check.

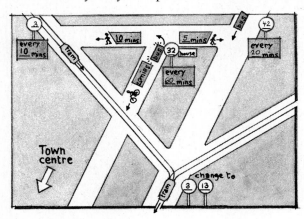

2 Working with the whole class the sentences should be collected on the board.

You might want to suggest phrases like: *... is more interesting than ... / ... is more dangerous than ... / ... is more exciting than ...* etc.

3 a After reading individually at their own speed encourage the students to scan the text for the information required in the true/false exercise.

True: 1, 3, 6, 7
False: 2, 4, 5, 8

i A *bus depot* in the US is a station where people get on and off the bus. It is also a terminal where buses are parked overnight.

Greyhound lines consist of about 4,500 buses which go nearly everywhere in the USA and in Canada. Greyhound lines connect almost every city and thousands of small towns. Buses are normally well equipped (e.g. with toilet, air-conditioning, tinted windows and reading lamps); they are clean, safe and comfortable.
In America, Greyhound buses are an accepted means of public transport which is normally cheaper than trains. However, it is not normally possible to reserve seats. It is recommended to be at the bus terminal at least 45 minutes before departure. If the bus happens to be full, an extra bus will be provided.
Greyhound buses run a 24-hour service weekdays and on public holidays. On long trips the journey can be broken a number of times. Long-distance buses stop at motorway services for the passengers to have a meal or a snack.
All buses use the same central bus stations in American cities, so that it is easy to change or connect bus lines.

Bus passes: Like the trains, bus lines offer passes. In the US a *Greyhound pass* for eight or fifteen days is available. With this people can travel almost as far as the Canadian border. The *Canada-Ameripass* is valid anywhere in Canada and the USA. There are seven, fifteen or thirty-day passes, all of which cost less than the train passes. Most lines offer various specials. There are no student or youth fares on buses, but for students there is a 14-trip booklet of tickets that gives a reduction.

In Great Britain there is a large network of bus routes served by various bus companies, such as: *Scottish Citylink, London Express, Londonlink, Transline* and *National Express,* one of the biggest. The British long-distance bus network goes to all major cities and is a particularly cheap and relatively fast way to travel. Apart from special price tariffs, there is the so-called *Britexpress Card.* This card entitles you to reductions of up to a third off the normal price of an unlimited number of journeys taken over 30 consecutive days, on all *National Express* bus routes in England and Wales, as well as on most *Scottish Citylink* journeys.
The *Britexpress Card* is available from travel agents, airports (*Heathrow, Gatwick*) and from *Victoria Coach Station,* the central bus station in London, upon presentation of a passport.

b To get the students started you could ask them about any experience they have had of people coming from abroad to their home, place of work, etc. and tell them of any personal experience you may have had. They may even be interested to talk about problems they have encountered due to lack of previous knowledge when travelling abroad. When they start making their suggestions you could help them by writing more sentence beginnings on the board, e.g. *It's a good idea to … / You may have to … / It's best to …*

Possible answers:
… take out health insurance.
… buy a railcard that allows you to travel cheaply.
… learn a few French phrases.
… try bed and breakfast accommodation.

Home study A

1 The Shakespeare Connection: travelling by train and bus
Extension Classroom: Talking about different ways of travelling

Students study a brochure describing a trip to Stratford-upon-Avon and answer questions. They listen to a dialogue at the train station and focus on the questions.

Vocabulary	depart, return ticket, single ticket
Functions	asking for information *When's the next/last …? / How long do I have to …? / How much …? /* *Can I reserve …? / What time does …? / Which platform …?*
Grammar	question words present simple (future meaning)
Skills	writing: writing questions reading: reading for specific information listening: listening for specific information

i

Stratford-upon-Avon is a busy English tourist town on the river Avon that has become famous as the birthplace of William Shakespeare. It is one of the oldest towns in England. The house where Shakespeare was born has been kept as a memorial. It is open to the public. At Shottery, 1 mile west of Stratford, you can visit the thatched cottage that was the home of Anne Hathaway, his wife. Each summer, a Shakespeare festival is held in Stratford. England's leading actors perform in Shakespeare's plays during this festival which lasts from April to November each year.

The *Britrail pass* is a special cheap ticket for travelling by train in Britain. The Britrail pass cannot, however, be obtained in Britain. It is therefore important to ask about this in one's own country, for example at main railway stations, travel agencies or a BTA (British Tourist Authority) office.

2 Checking in at the airport
Extension   Classroom: Talking about different ways of travelling

Students listen to a woman checking in for a flight, answer questions and focus on important vocabulary. They also listen to announcements and decide what to do.

Vocabulary	at least, business class, flight, gate, immediately, seat *(n.)*, section*
Functions	asking for information *How much ...? / How many ...? / When's the next ...? / Can I ...? /* *What's ...? / When'll ...? / Will there be ...?*
Grammar	question words present simple (future meaning)
Skills	listening: listening for specific information

3 Travelling across the USA
Extension   Classroom: Seeing the USA by bus

Students become familiar with a typical bus schedule and follow the bus route across the US answering questions along the way.

Vocabulary	abbreviation*, desert *(n.)*, to be located, state *(n.)*, time zone*
Grammar	questions
Skills	reading: reading for specific information

i

Washington D.C.: D.C. stands for *District of Columbia*. The District of Columbia is not a state itself. To avoid any misunderstanding, it is common to say *Washington State* when talking about the *state of Washington*. The same is true for *New York City* and *New York State*.

USA and *US* are used as abbreviations for the United States. US is more common.

Classroom B

Students talk about America, working on facts they already know. They exchange opinions about what would interest them in the US.

◄ ►

Grammar	*If*-clause (hypothetical condition)
Skills	speaking: brainstorming vocabulary and making suggestions to categorize it
	writing: completing sentences, writing statements to reinforce the grammar point
	reading: reading short texts which support the grammar point
	listening: listening to sentences written by other students in order to identify who wrote them

Procedure

1 a Allow the pairs plenty of time to brainstorm AMERICA. Go round helping with spelling, but do not make suggestions. Each pair should write down at least twenty words.

Possible answers:
Statue of Liberty, Big Apple, hamburgers, Disneyland, freedom, jazz, Rockies, friendly, American English, Hollywood, skyscrapers, open, busy, California, immigration restrictions, contrasts, big cars, gold rush, fast food, long distances, the American Dream, green card, etc.

b The students write the words they get from another pair in two columns under FACT and OPINION.

Possible answer:

FACT	OPINION
Statue of Liberty	open
Big Apple	freedom
hamburgers	busy
Disneyland	friendly
…	…

c Give the students time to read and comment on the classifications. With a good class you could start a discussion on prejudice and stereotypes and ask them, for example, *What would Americans say about your country?*

2 The students work individually. They go to the board and write down the sentence they have found from memory. An alternative would be to turn this activity into a little competition. For example, the winner is the first person who manages to write down a correct sentence / manages to make up the longest sentence, etc.

Possible answers:
If I went to the USA, I'd try to meet American families.
If I went to the USA, I'd rent a camper.
If I went to the USA, I'd try hamburgers.
If I went to the USA, I'd go to the Rockies.

i *Motels* offer overnight accommodation usually in self-contained units with attached car-parking facilities. Breakfast or other meals are not normally provided.

3 a A silent reading task. Then ask students to close their books and try to remember what the children would do. Collect the information on the board in the following way: *If I won a trip, I'd fly to New York. If I won a trip, I'd like to see the dolphins.*

i *Indian Country* refers to the reservations where most of the Indian population live. *Goofy* is a dog-like character created by Walt Disney.

b Get the students to complete the sentences individually.

1. won … I'd go   2. won … I'd try … I'd visit   3. won … I'd take   4. won … I'd fly

4 Ask the students to write their sentences on a sheet of paper. Collect the papers and redistribute them making sure no one gets his/her own paper. Get them to read the sentences they receive and let the others speculate who may have written them.
An alternative would be to let the students read the sentences, telling who wrote them and getting others in the group to comment using phrases such as: *So would I. / Why not? / That's a brilliant idea. / I'd never do that. / I wouldn't mind that either.*

Photocopy the word roses on page 126 for the following lesson (C-Block, exercise 1).

Home study B

1 Travelling around the USA
Extension   Classroom: Comparing ways of transport (C7A/2)

Students read advertisements for different ways of travelling and then listen to Jenny giving travel advice to Bruce.

Vocabulary	besides, comfortable, convenient*, fun, headline*, inexpensive, relaxing*, reliable*, rent (*v.*), safe (*adj.*), timetable
Functions	comparing things *… as fast/good as … / … is faster/safer than … / … is more comfortable/convenient/expensive/interesting/relaxing/reliable than … / the best way to …*
Grammar	comparison of adjectives modal verb: *will* (promise)
Skills	writing: writing personal statements reading: reading for specific information listening: listening for specific information

2 Going west
Extension   Classroom: Talking about holidays (C6B, C)

Students listen to Jenny talking about a trip her family made across the US when she was a child and pick out words that express feelings and emotions.

Vocabulary	disappointed, embarrassed, excited, expect, happy, sad, scared*, terribly bored
Functions	talking about feelings *We were very excited. / I was sad to … / I was disappointed when … / We were terribly bored … / We were all happy … / I was pleased to … / I was relieved. / I would have been too embarrassed … / We were surprised when …*
Grammar	past simple past perfect
Skills	listening: listening for specific information

3 Signs
Extension   Classroom: Traffic signs (C3B / 1d)

Students interpret public signs.

Vocabulary	allow, climb, except, pool *(n.)*, supposed to, wall, watch out for
Functions	forbidding *You are not supposed to … / You are not allowed to … / Do not …*
Grammar	modal verbs: *have to* (obligation, necessity) *(be) allowed to* (instead of *can* or *may*) imperative
Skills	reading: reading for specific information

Classroom C

Students revise expressions connected with the seasons and the weather.

◀ ▶

Grammar	future: *be + going to* + infinitive (plan, intention) *will/'ll* (prediction)
Skills	speaking: discussing word associations, definitions and categorizations writing: writing a weather forecast reading: reading what another student has written and commenting on it listening: listening and noting down future tense forms

Procedure

1 Distribute the photocopies of the word roses from page 126.
Go round helping students with unknown vocabulary as they ask for it. In groups of four let them look at the other students' word roses and collect any new vocabulary. Students then talk about their favourite seasons.

Possible answers:

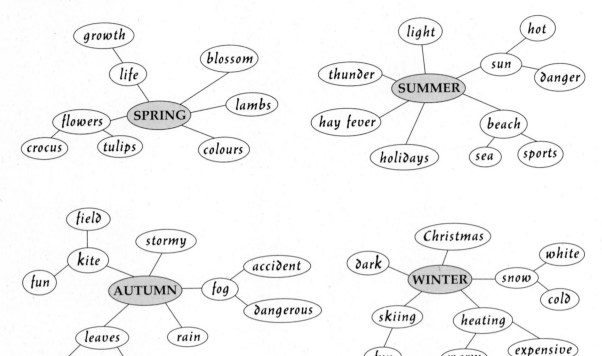

2 a Ask the students to give reasons.

summer

b This can be done with the whole class or in pairs.

1. no – steady rain
3. yes – occasional rain
2. yes – calm and sunny
4. no – strong winds

3 a, b, c Let the students work individually and use the *going to* or *will* forms from the weather map. For additional explanation on the use of *going to* and *will* refer to the grammar on page 223 in the Student's Book.

a 1. Sooner or later it**'s going to** rain.
2. It **is also going to turn** quite windy in the west.
3. During the afternoon and evening it **will start to rain** in eastern England and Scotland.

4. London and the SE **will escape** the worst of the rain, but further north and west some of it **will be** heavy.
5. These breezy areas **will see** a change to drier and slightly brighter weather.

b 1. Manchester
2. London
3. Birmingham

c 1. I'm afraid **it's going to rain** for most of the day.
2. Some of the rain **will be** heavy.
3. It**'ll be** cool, as well.
4. The day here **will have** a bright start.
5. There **will be** occasional rain.
6. We **are not going to see** the sun today.
7. It **will be** dull all day and there **will be** intermittent rain.
8. It**'ll be** no warmer than 17 degrees.

d The weather forecast should not be more than two or three sentences and you should go round correcting individually as much as possible.

Possible answer:
It is going to start out bright with clouds moving in from the west by noon. Showers during the afternoon will die out giving a dry evening. Temperatures will remain well below the seasonal average ranging from 14°C in the north to 17°C in the south.

e The students can either write down their plans for the weekend on the paper they receive, or this can be done orally. Make sure they use a form of the future tense.

4 **a** Put the students into two groups. Group A looks at File 13 on page 213 and group B looks at File 20 on page 215. In a class of more than ten divide the students into two A groups and two B groups. Recommend students discuss fully which words could best be drawn, translated, etc. before they actually start on the task. Two words from each file can be omitted as the students wish.
While the students are preparing the definitions, translations, drawings and opposites for the other group, go round making sure they do not write the words from their file on the paper.

File 13 (page 213)

Group A				
clouds	autumn	sun	snow	intermittent
cool	bright	windy	lightning	dry

File 20 (page 215)

Group B				
rain	degrees	dull	warm	forecast
thunder	slightly	occasional	wet	breezy

Possible answers:
File 13
clouds:

cool: warm
autumn: the season after summer
bright: dull
sun:

snow: Schnee
lightning: very bright flashes of light in the sky during a thunderstorm
dry: trocken

(*intermittent* and *windy* have been left out)

File 20
rain:

thunder: the loud noise that you hear in the sky after a flash of lightning
degrees:

dull: trübe
warm: cold
wet: dry
forecast: Vorhersage
breezy: a fairly strong but pleasant wind

(*slightly* and *occasional* have been left out)

b Students exchange papers and try to work out the words from the other group's list. When the words have been found you can round off the lesson with a general discussion on the best ways of noting down vocabulary.

Home study C

1 A day in the life of two tourists in San Francisco
Extension Classroom: Talking about holidays (C6B, C)

Students read a newspaper article about how a couple spent a day in San Francisco.

Vocabulary	advise, carefully, choose, discover, discuss, examine, exit (*v.*), explore, normally, polite, suggest
Grammar	present perfect future: *be + going to +* infinitive (plan, intention)
Skills	reading: reading for information; reading for specific information

i

Gumps is an expensive department store that is supposed to have everything a person could want.

Napa Valley, which is north of San Francisco, is the centre of the Californian wine industry. Most of the finest wineries are located here.

Sausalito is an affluent, avant-garde residential town on the other side of the Golden Gate Bridge which attracts many tourists and has lots of art galleries, craft shops, restaurants and cafés.

Broadway is famous for its night clubs. This is where the first topless club opened in the US.

2 The weather
Review Classroom: Talking about the weather

Students review weather vocabulary by finding words that describe weather conditions in a wordsearch puzzle.

Vocabulary	bright, cloudy, cool, dull, fair, freezing, rainy, shower *(n.)* snowy, sunny, thunder *(n.)*
Grammar	word formation (adjectives)
Skills	reading: reading for specific information; reading for enjoyment

3 Hurricane Charley
Extension Classroom: Talking about the weather (C7C/1–4)

Students read a text about what happened when a terrific storm hit Britain and listen to the newsreport on the radio.

Vocabulary	block *(v.)*, body, cause *(v.)*, drown*, expert, heavily, helicopter*, motorist, power-cut, rescue*
Grammar	passive future: *will/'ll* (prediction)
Skills	reading: reading for specific information listening: listening for information; listening for specific information

Unit 8 · Free time

Classroom A

Students exchange ideas and opinions about hobbies and free-time activities.

◄►

Grammar	present simple with frequency adverbs present perfect modal verb: *used to* (to express a former habit/state)
Skills	speaking: collecting and presenting facts about other students listening: listening for specific information

Procedure

1 a Get the students to read the questions first so they know what information they have to listen out for.

1. a lot   2. quite a lot   3. hardly any   4. not so much   5. a lot   6. no time at all

b Make sure the students use the question *How much time do you spend …?* If necessary, put the question on the board.

2 a Get the students to read out the answers. Encourage them to repeat the information, e.g. *The speaker never goes dancing. The speaker hardly ever goes to a club.*

1. never
2. hardly ever
3. quite often
4. once a month
5. every Tuesday evening
6. occasionally
7. quite often
8. hardly ever
9. sometimes
10. jogging: three times a week; swimming: often
11. quite often

b Write the question the students should use on the board *How often do you …?* Give them a time limit, e.g. five minutes, and let them ask as many different questions as they want to using the sentences (1–8) in the exercise or others that occur to them. Students write down the person's name and the information they get from him/her.

c Every student should report back at least one piece of information. Afterwards get them to recollect from memory pieces of information they heard. You can make this into a competition by asking who can remember the most, e.g. *Inge never goes to concerts. Peter often goes to a restaurant.*

3 a Tell the students to do this exercise in the form of a table (see page 153 in the Student's Book). Point out that some sports can occur under different headings, depending on how they are interpreted. For example, riding could also be classed as a team sport, an indoor sport and a sport where points can be scored. Football can also be played indoors, beach volleyball outdoors, etc. Encourage quicker students to work on more than one sport.

Possible answer:

1. sports involving a ball:	volleyball, football, cricket, rugby, tennis
2. team sports:	volleyball, football, cricket, rugby
3. sports involving a partner:	tennis
4. water sports:	sailing, surfing
5. sports involving an animal:	riding
6. indoor sports:	volleyball, tennis
7. outdoor sports:	tennis, football, cricket, sailing, skiing, surfing, riding
8. sports where points or goals can be scored:	volleyball, football, cricket, rugby, tennis
9. Olympic disciplines:	volleyball, tennis, riding, skiing, sailing

Cricket is an outdoor game played between two teams, each consisting of eleven people. Players try to score points, called *runs*, by hitting a ball with a wooden bat. Players traditionally wear white clothes.

Rugby: There are two types of rugby: *Rugby League* (professional sport) and *Rugby Union* (amateur sport). The most popular is *Rugby Union*, a game of two teams, each with 15 players. The ball is oval-shaped. The players wear no special protection, their clothes are similar to footballers'. The ball must be carried over the opposing team's baseline and placed on the ground in order to score a *try* (4 points). There are possible points for a *conversion* if the ball is then kicked between both posts and over the crossbar. Further points can be scored through *penalties* (3 points) and *drop-goals* (3 points). The team is made up of 8 *forwards* and 7 *backs*. The job of the *forwards* is to gain possession of the ball so that the *backs* can run with it.

In American English, football is called *soccer*.

American football is a game with two teams, each with 11 players, who have to get the egg-shaped ball across the opposing team's baseline. The ball can be carried, thrown or kicked. The players wear head and mouth protection and padding round the lower body, on the shoulders and knee-joints. Physical tackles on opposing players are allowed, for example throwing the opponent to the ground or tackling his legs, blocking him; the tackle must, however, come from the front. The biggest competitions in the USA are called *Bowls*, for example professional football's *Super-Bowl*.

b The students work individually. They can compare their answers with a partner.

cooking	F
dancing	E
drawing / painting	D
knitting	A
singing	H
photography	B
sewing	G
playing a guitar	C

c Give an example yourself of a hobby you do regularly, e.g. *I often sew clothes for my family*. Give an example of a hobby you have tried, e.g. *I used to sing in a choir, but I don't any more*. Finally, give an example of a hobby you have never tried, but would like to, e.g. *I've never done photography, but I'd like to try*. Put all three sentences on the board. Let the students work in groups on their own sentences and go round checking on the correct tense use. They can use other hobbies than those in 3b, if they wish.

4 a Individually the students match the pictures.

blues	5
jazz	2
classical	6
pop	3
folk	4
rock	1

b Read out some of the students' lists and let the class try to guess who wrote them.

 Photocopy the newspaper articles on page 127 for the next lesson (B-Block, exercise 3b). Also ask students to bring in the latest German and English newspapers (B-Block, exercise 4).

Home study A

1 Crossword
Extension   Classroom: Talking about hobbies and interests (C8A/1–4)

Students review and learn new vocabulary by filling in a crossword.

Vocabulary	classic (n.)*, comedy*, non-fiction*, politics, relationship, stage show, star (v.), story, thriller*, western*
Skills	reading: reading for specific information; reading for enjoyment

2 Can you …?
Extension   Classroom: Talking about sports, hobbies and interests (C8A/1–4)

Students listen to a woman talking about her hobbies and focus on answering questions.

Vocabulary	actually, bit (n.), hopeless
Functions	expressing ability *I'm quite good at …, actually. / I'm quite a good …, actually. / I can … a bit. / I can't … very well. / I'm absolutely hopeless at … / I've never really tried. / I've forgotten how. / I've never learned.*
Grammar	modal verb: *can* (ability) present perfect
Skills	writing: writing personal statements listening: listening for specific information; listening and responding

3 Likes and dislikes
Extension   Classroom: Talking about interests (C8A/1–4)

Students listen to a woman talking about what sort of entertainment she likes and pick out ways of expressing likes and dislikes.

Vocabulary	stand (v.), otherwise
Functions	expressing likes and dislikes *I love … / I enjoy … / I like some … / I don't mind … / I prefer … / I don't think much of … / I don't like … much. / I can't stand …*
Skills	writing: writing personal statements listening: listening for specific information; listening and responding

4 What's on in San Francisco?
Extension   Classroom: Travelling and making suggestions (C7A/3)

Students look at an entertainment guide and listen to a dialogue where they are asked to pick out the suggestions.

Vocabulary	documentary*, keen on doing s.th.
Functions	making suggestions and accepting/rejecting *Why don't we …? / What about …? / Shall we …? / We could … / How about …? / Let's … / That's fine with me. / Great. / I'm not too keen on … / That's a good idea. / To be honest, I'd rather not. / Yes, let's.*
Grammar	modal verbs: *could* (suggestion) *shall* (suggestion)
Skills	reading: reading for specific information listening: listening for specific information

Classroom B

Students have the opportunity to read newspaper articles, to give their ideas and opinions on the media and to learn about the British press.

Grammar	present simple present continuous

Skills	speaking: answering questions and developing a conversation;
	          discussing and speculating on vocabulary;
	          talking about stories in the news
	writing: note taking
	reading: skimming and scanning texts;
	          reading questions aloud
	listening: listening for factual information from the cassette;
	          listening to each other to share opinions

Procedure

1 **a** Make sure the students understand 'serious' and 'tabloid' by giving examples of newspapers they know. They work individually and mark the table as they listen.

	serious	tabloid	left-wing	centre	right-wing
Daily Express		✓			✓
The Guardian	✓		✓		
The Independent	✓			✓	
Daily Mail		✓			✓
Daily Mirror		✓	✓		
Daily Star		✓			✓
The Sun		✓			✓
The Daily Telegraph	✓				✓
The Times	✓				✓
Today		✓			✓
The Observer	✓		✓		
Sunday Telegraph	✓				✓
The Sunday Times	✓				✓

The British Press: Fleet Street used to signify the place where England's newspapers were printed and edited. However, since the 1980's different newspaper groups have been bought and sold, often by overseas multi-media magnates such as the Australian entrepreneur *Rupert Murdoch*, which in turn has radically changed the face of the British press. The aim of these financially powerful businessmen was to introduce the most up to date computer printing techniques, which would require only a limited number of personnel. The trade unions vehemently opposed this move but, eventually, the biggest printing union SOGAT 82 *(Society of Graphical and Allied Trades)* gave up the fight against Rupert Murdoch *(News International)*. Rupert Murdoch owns *News International* in Wapping (the East End of London) where he publishes *The Times, The Sun* and *The News of the World*. The newspaper revolution with its new technology swept most newspaper headquarters out of Fleet Street to other locations where they can operate their plant more efficiently.

b Before they attempt this exercise the students will probably need to hear the cassette a second time. After they have worked on their own they can compare answers with a partner.

pictures of topless models
stories about the royal family
stories about TV soap operas

2 In pairs student A looks at File 14 on page 213 and student B looks at File 19 on page 215. Stress that students should ask the questions alternately. Finally, you can get the students to report back one or two interesting things they may have heard.

File 14 (page 213)

Student A
1. Which newspaper do you read daily?
2. What sections interest you most?
3. Which sections do you never read?
4. Which foreign newspapers or magazines have you ever read?
5. What do you think about the news on TV and programmes about current affairs?

File 19 (page 215)

Student B
1. Do you ever read a weekly newspaper or magazine?
2. What do you read first in the newspaper?
3. Are any of the sections of no interest to you?
4. What do you think about the news on the radio?
5. How well informed do you think you are?

3 a Students work in pairs. Go round helping with vocabulary, but do not make any suggestions yourself. Get the students to supplement their lists using the vocabulary from other pairs.

b Hand out the newspaper articles you have photocopied from page 127. Either individually or in pairs students skim the texts for global understanding and match the headlines. Then they scan the texts to find the words they had predicted. These can be underlined or highlighted. Students can then silently read the text again to focus on the content.

Young offenders to be locked up for twice as long B
Man dies in bid to halt gunman   C
Vitamin pills take on preventive role   A

4 Brainstorm the main news stories and if necessary make notes on the board. Students might want to have a look at the newspapers they have brought to class. They then enter the stories under the correct headings. Point out to them that one news item can occur under several different headings. For example "Attack on African President" can come under the headings POLITICAL NEWS, INTERNATIONAL NEWS and CRIME. "Explosion at a German Chemical Plant" can be put under HOME NEWS and ACCIDENTS OR DISASTER.

Home study B

1 Reading the newspaper
Extension Classroom: Talking about newspapers (C8B/1–4)

Students read the contents page of a newspaper and decide what they would expect to find in certain sections. Then they match headlines with sections of the paper.

Vocabulary	art, content*, detail, for sale, home news, overseas news*, property
Skills	reading: reading for information; reading for specific information

> **i** *Bridge* is a popular card game in Britain and in the US played with four people. The players bid or have to say how many tricks they are going to win before they play their cards. If they bid correctly, they win points.

2 Sports and fitness
Extension Classroom: Sports (C8A/2, 3)

Students listen to three people talking about how they stay fit and write about their own fitness habits.

Vocabulary	exercise class, exhausted *(adj.)*, hike*, race *(n.)*, regularly
Grammar	present perfect continuous modal verb: *used to* (to express a former habit/state)
Skills	writing: writing personal statements listening: listening for specific information

3 An interview
Review Classroom: Free-time activities

Students match the questions to the answers in an interview on free-time activities.

Grammar	questions
Skills	reading: reading for information

Classroom C

Students continue talking about free time and read from George Orwell's essay *The Moon under Water*, which is about an ideal pub.

◀ ▶

Functions	agreeing and disagreeing
	I agree (completely). / I (totally) disagree. / I neither agree nor disagree.
Grammar	present simple
Skills	speaking: exchange of ideas about free-time activities;
	expressing opinions about a variety of topics connected with free time;
	talking about the content of the text
	reading: reading to encourage comment and discussion

Procedure

1 a You might want to start the students off by telling them the activities you do regularly, e.g. *I go jogging*. Then get them to ask you questions, *e.g. When do you go? / Where do you go? / How long do you spend jogging?*

b Work with those students who do not find a partner in the group, but encourage them to ask each other questions rather than you taking over an interviewing role.

2 a Give the students enough time to complete the task. Make sure everybody has marked every statement. Go round and check thoroughly.

b With a large class divide the students into groups of four or five, but with less than eight have a class discussion. Move on to a new topic as soon as you notice that the discussion is beginning to flag.

3 a Tell the students to read the text silently to understand the content. During a second reading they can underline any expressions they find difficult. Encourage them to guess meaning from the context and then to talk to others about difficult words. They can complete the exercise individually or in pairs.

The food is good.	7
It is not too small.	4
The barmaids are nice.	6
It is old-fashioned.	3/4
It is quiet.	5/1
There is a garden.	8
What is the best thing about the pub?	the garden
Why?	because whole families can go there

i

In Great Britain the *pub* (short for *public house*) is a traditional feature of almost every town and village, and is often a building of character or historic interest. It is an establishment where both alcoholic and non-alcoholic drinks are sold and snacks are normally available. Many pubs nowadays have more to offer, with extensive lunchtime and evening menus, live music and other entertainments. Some also offer accommodation. Most pubs open twice daily, over lunchtime and in the evening, and some now open all day, from 11 a.m. to 11 p.m. All pubs have distinctive names, many of which reflect their historic origin.

Drinks and meals are ordered at the bar and paid for straight away. Groups of friends usually take it in turns to buy a *round*, i.e. each person in turn buys the drinks for the others. The barman normally warns customers ten minutes before closing time by calling *Last orders!*, ringing a bell or dimming the lights. Customers may then order one last drink. Then, at 11 p.m., the barman will ring a bell and call *Time, ladies and gentlemen, please!* to announce that the pub is about to close.

George Orwell was born in Bengal in 1903. He saw himself primarily as a political writer, a democratic socialist who was to become more and more disillusioned with the methods of Communism. His first novel *Burmese Days* was published in 1934. In *The Road to Wigan Pier* (1937) he gives a vivid and impassioned documentary of unemployment and proletarian life in the north of England. His plain colloquial style made him highly effective as a journalist and he contributed regularly to several London newspapers. His most popular novels were *Animal Farm* (1945) and *Nineteen eighty-four* (1949). He died in 1950 of tuberculosis, which he had suffered from for many years.

b Get the students to supplement their lists from those of other students.

Possible answers:
the bus stop, the fire, the ladies' bar, the pub entertainments, aspirins and stamps, the food, the old-fashioned money (shillings)

Home study C

1 The Moon under Water
Extension Classroom: Pubs (C8C/3)

Students listen to Bruce comparing pubs today with those of many years ago and focus on communicating ideas and information.

Vocabulary	apparently*, constant*, doubt *(v.)*, generally, legal*, mention *(v.)*, officially, suspect *(v.)**
Functions	expressing certainty and uncertainty *I don't know … / I don't suppose … / I (don't) think … / I doubt … / I'm sure … / I suspect …*
Skills	listening: listening for information; listening for specific information

2 Pub crossword
Review   Classroom: The Moon under Water (C8C/3)

Students review vocabulary by filling in a crossword.

Vocabulary	round (*n.*)
Skills	reading: reading for specific information; reading for enjoyment

3 Watching TV in Britain and the USA
Extension   Classroom: Free-time activities

Students look at different types of TV programmes and listen to an interview about TV in Britain and the USA.

Vocabulary	channel*, commercial*, control (*v.*), educational (*adj.*), government, series*
Skills	reading: reading for information; reading for specific information listening: listening for specific information

Unit 9 · Home and environment

Classroom A

Students learn new vocabulary to describe houses and homes and look at typical houses in Britain.

◀ ▶

Grammar	present perfect future: *be + going to* + infinitive *there + be*
Skills	speaking: using language of description to communicate accurate factual information; using language of description to give accurate factual information as well as trying to create the right atmosphere writing: a creative drill to support the grammar point reading: reading to check understanding of basic vocabulary items needed for the unit (*detached, semi-detached, terrace, town house*) and to learn about typical houses in Britain listening: global listening for content; listening for detailed information; listening to reinforce the grammar point

Procedure

1 **a** The students work individually. Ask them if they would like to live in house A and why or why not.

type of house: semi-detached
number of bedrooms: 2
other rooms: lounge, dining room, morning room, fitted kitchen, bathroom, cellars
car-parking facilities: detached garage
garden(s): attractive front and back gardens
central heating: yes

In Britain people tend to move house several times during their life. They often buy and sell their houses, moving into a larger or smaller property to suit their present family situation. There are four common house types in Britain:

Detached house: A house standing on its own land and not attached to another building.
Semi(-detached house): A house attached on one side only to another, usually very similar, house.
Terraced house: A (usually small) house that is one of a continuous row in one block in a street. Many rows of terraced houses were originally built for workers in nearby factories or coal mines.
Block of flats: A large building containing a number of flats.

b The students read silently and underline any words they do not know. They can ask you and each other for unknown vocabulary before the matching activity.

1. picture E   2. picture D   3. picture B   4. picture C

c Let the students listen to the cassette and work out the answer. Students can work in pairs.

House A
Reasons: It is the only house with cellars, two bedrooms and an upstairs bathroom/toilet.

2 a Students listen to the dialogue and complete the task. With a good class get the students to try the exercise from memory before the second listening.

bathroom	6
bedrooms	7
breakfast room/morning room	5
cellar	8
dining room	3
hall	1
kitchen	4
lounge/living room	2

b Students listen to the dialogue and complete the task with the help of a table. With a good class get the students to try the exercise from memory before they listen to the cassette again. Then give them time to supplement what they have written.

Hall:	We haven't decorated it yet.
Lounge:	We're going to paint the walls this weekend. We're going to keep the curtains. We've ordered a new carpet.
Dining room:	We haven't done anything in here. We've bought a new table.
Front bedroom:	We're going to repaint the front bedroom.
Bathroom/Toilet:	We're not going to change anything yet.
Cellar:	We've set up the workshop down there. We're going to build a games room.

3 Begin by describing the view from your window. With a weak class draw their attention to 'there is' and 'there are'. Stress the students should try to create the atmosphere evoked by the view.

Possible answer:
From my living room window I can see a large garden. There are several fruit trees, flowers and bushes and a small pond. Behind the wooden garden fence there is a public path, and at the weekend people often go for a walk along here. At the far side of this path is a ditch, which in winter is sometimes filled with water. Beyond the ditch are meadows where you can see rabbits, foxes and even deer.

4 a Before students set out to describe their living room, stress they keep to the facts. If you feel students would be unhappy about describing their room, get them to describe a fictitious living room.

b Go round making sure the structures (present perfect / *be* + *going to* + infinitive) are used correctly.

c As an alternative you might want to turn this activity into a drill. Students read out two sentences they have produced in 4b. After each student has had his/her turn, they reconstruct from memory what was said by the whole class.

Home study A

1 Where is it?
Review   Classroom: Saying where things are (C3A/1)

Students look at a picture of a spare room filled with common household items and complete sentences that describe where the things are.

Vocabulary	alarm clock*, bookshelf, cooker, cupboard, freezer, fridge*, kettle*, lamp, record player, saucepan*, sink (n.), typewriter, wardrobe*, washbasin*
Functions	saying where things are *s.th. is at the bottom / at the top / in the middle (of) / on the left/ right / behind / between / in / in front of / next to / on / on top of / under / at / near / with*
Grammar	prepositions
Skills	reading: reading for information

2 Moving house
Extension   Classroom: Talking about houses (C9A/1, 2, 4)

Students listen to Bruce talking about where he has lived and why he moved from one place to another. Students take notes and complete sentences.

Vocabulary	cleaner (n.), share (v.)
Functions	giving reasons *... because ...*
Grammar	word order: questions prepositions
Skills	writing: note taking listening: listening for specific information

3 Murder at the farm
Extension   Classroom: Talking about houses (C9A/1, 2, 4)

Students read the clues in order to solve the mystery and decide who was in the room at the time of the murder.

Grammar	past continuous
Skills	reading: reading for specific information

▬ Classroom B ▬▬▬▬▬▬▬▬▬▬▬▬▬▬▬▬▬▬▬▬▬▬▬▬

Students consider the idea of home sharing or living in a commune and talk about the advantages and disadvantages of living together.

◄ ►

Skills	speaking:	role play involving interviewing, evaluating and coming to a conclusion
	listening:	listening to interviews for specific information and as a stimulus for further discussion

Procedure

1 Put the students into five groups. With less than ten students make three or four groups, ensuring that one group gets file E. You can then choose any of the files from A to D for the remaining groups. Give the students enough time to work out their situation. Help with vocabulary if necessary, but try not to interfere with their decision making. With a good class you could play one of the roles yourself. Make sure the students from group E are interviewed by each of the other groups.

☞ Where two of the following files appear on a doublespread page, make sure that the students cover the file they do not need.

File 2 (page 210)

> **Group A**
> You live in a commune. You are students and are looking for a new member to share your flat. Decide about your age, interests and life style and the sort of person you are looking for.

File 7 (page 211)

> **Group B**
> You live in a commune. You are young professionals and are looking for a new member to share your house. Decide about your age, interests and life style and the sort of person you are looking for.

File 11 (page 212)

> **Group C**
> You live in a commune. You are a group of people who are concerned about ecology and the environment and are looking for a new member to share your house and large garden. Decide about your age, interests and life style and the sort of person you are looking for.

File 16 (page 214)

Group D
You live in a commune. You are a group of elderly people and are looking for a new member to share your house. Decide about your age, interests and life style and the sort of person you are looking for.

File 21 (page 215)

Group E
You are all individuals who are looking for a place in a commune. Decide about your needs, what duties you would be prepared to do and the sort of people you would like to live with.

2 Give the students enough time to read the instructions before playing the cassette. Stop the cassette at the bell and allow them to mark true or false.
They then continue with the cassette until they hear the next bell. They again complete the task individually.
Do not correct or comment before the students listen to the third part of the interview and have marked the final true and false.
Then get the students to compare their answers and if they have problems, you may need to play parts of the interview again.

First part of the interview
True: 2, 3
False: 1

Second part of the interview
Shirley: b, c, e, g, h
Anne: a, d, f, i

Third part of the interview
True: 4, 5
False: 6

3 If the students just say *yes* or *no* go round encouraging them to give reasons for their answers. If there is enough interest or there are students in the group with personal experience of home sharing, it would be worthwhile to have a class discussion.

═ Home study B ═

1 Project SHARE
Review   Classroom: Interview with two people participating in Project SHARE (C9B/2)

Students listen to the interview (from C9B/2) again and complete sentences.

Vocabulary	raise a family*, widow*
Functions	talking about feelings *I was afraid … / I was nervous about … / I was worried that … / I'm very happy with … / I'm happy for … / We're all very pleased with … / I'm not afraid … / I don't have to worry about …*
Grammar	reflexive pronouns
Skills	listening: listening for specific information

2 What's it called?
Review   Classroom/Home study: Talking about houses (C9A/1–3; H9A/2)

Students label a picture of a house and its fittings with words that are given in a box.

Vocabulary	basket*, bookcase*, carpet*, dishwasher, fireplace*, mixer, quilt*, rug*
Skills	writing: labelling

3 The price of housing
Extension   Classroom: Houses in Britain (C9A/1; H9A/2)

Students read three texts on the housing market and pick out information and vocabulary.

Vocabulary	accommodation*, afford, appeal (n.)*, authority*, average, boom*, council (n.)*, depressing*, desirable*, desperate*, divide*, evidence*, increase (v., n.), job-seeker*, major (adj.)*, mobility*, rise (n.), shortage*, unemployment, unique*, vacancy*
Skills	reading: reading for information; reading for specific information

Classroom C

Students discuss pollution in general and focus on the increase in noise levels.

◄►
> **Skills**   speaking: asking and answering questions;
> commenting on the opinions of others;
> discussing vocabulary to produce definitions
>
> reading: reading to confirm predictions about content;
> reading to match one-sentence summaries to each paragraph

Procedure

1 In pairs student A looks at File 15 on page 213 and student B looks at File 22 on page 215. Then get the students to report back to the whole class anything interesting they have heard from their partner and try to develop a class discussion.

File 15 (page 213)

> **Student A**
> 1. What is pollution?
> 2. Was there pollution 200 years ago?
> 3. What do you think the government is doing to control pollution?
> 4. Should there be a tax on all packaging?
> 5. Is it realistic to think that environmental problems can be solved?

File 22 (page 215)

> **Student B**
> 1. When was the problem of pollution first recognized?
> 2. What different kinds of pollution can we distinguish?
> 3. How can people be made aware of the problem?
> 4. Could public transport ever be efficient and cheap enough to replace cars in cities?
> 5. Is concern about the environment only of interest to a small section of the population?

2 **a** Students individually mark the statements true or false. They can then check their answers with others before silently reading the text in the Student's Book on page 185.

True: 1, 4, 7
False: 2, 3, 5, 6

b Let the students work individually or in pairs as they wish.

1 g   2 f   3 a   4 d   5 b   6 c   7 e

3 Put the class into two groups. With more than ten students make subgroups. Group A looks at File 6 on page 211 and group B looks at File 18 on page 214. On a separate sheet of paper they write clues for the filled-in crossword in their file. Remind the students that the clues can be translations, drawings, definitions, synonyms, antonyms or model sentences. They should try to decide in their group on the best technique for each word. When the students have written their clues they pass them to the group who was working on the other file. They use the clues they receive to fill in their empty crossword in the Student's Book on page 184.

File 6 (page 211)

Group A

Across →

4 _____

_____

6 _____

_____

7 _____

_____

8 _____

_____

Down ↓

1 _____

2 _____

3 _____

5 _____

Crossword grid (Group A):

							³P		
¹C						O		
L			²C		⁴L	O	⁵U	D
E			A		L		N	
A		⁶G	R	O	U	N	D	
N			P		T		E	
E			E		⁷E	A	R	N
⁸C	R	E	A	T	E	D		

File 18 (page 214)

Group B

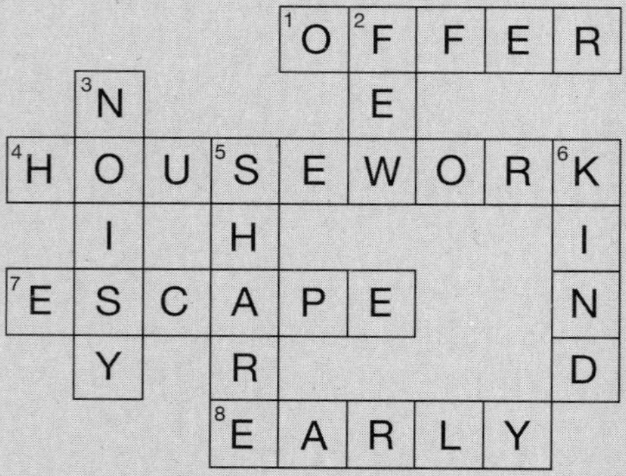

Across →

1 _____

_____

4 _____

_____

7 _____

_____

8 _____

_____

Down ↓

2 _____

3 _____

5 _____

6 _____

Crossword grid (Group B):

				¹O	²F	F	E	R
	³N				E			
⁴H	O	U	⁵S	E	W	O	R	⁶K
	I		H					I
⁷E	S	C	A	P	E			N
	Y		R					D
			⁸E	A	R	L	Y	

Possible answers:
File 6

Across →
4 she shouted so … that the neighbours could hear her
6 we walk on this every day
7 when you work for a company you … money
8 another word for 'made'

Down ↓
1 someone you employ to clean your house
2 a thick covering for the floors in your house
3 the air is becoming more and more … by cars and factories
5 the opposite of 'over'

File 18

Across →
1 if you want to help someone you … them a hand
4 one word which means doing the hoovering, dusting, cleaning, etc. at home
7 to manage to get away from somewhere, e.g. prison
8 a proverb: the … bird catches the worm

Down ↓
2 the opposite of 'lots'
3 similar to 'loud'
5 if two people divide something equally between themselves they … it
6 to be helpful and friendly to others

Home study C

1 Noise pollution
Review   Classroom: Article on noise pollution (C9B/2)

Students read the article *Noise: Getting louder all the time* again and match the beginnings of sentences to the endings. They complete a puzzle with the important vocabulary from the article.

Vocabulary	complaint, deal with, disturb, enforce*, overcrowded, prevent, produce *(v.)*, punish, responsible*, rush hour, thick
Grammar	passive
Skills	reading: reading for specific information

2 Noise makers
Extension   Classroom: Talking about noise pollution

Students decide what kinds of noise annoy them and then listen to the song
A Quiet Place.

Vocabulary	argue, couple*, disagree*, drunk *(n.)*, fight *(v.)*, shout *(v.)*
Skills	reading: reading for specific information; reading for enjoyment listening: listening for specific information; listening for enjoyment

3 Creating a national preserve
New topic   Home study: The politics of environmentalism

Students read an article on different interest groups and their reasons for supporting or opposing a nature preserve.

Vocabulary	to be against *(adv.)*, cattle*, destroy, environmentalist, fear *(n.)*, grow, notice *(n.)*, promise *(v.)*, solve, support *(v.)*, threaten, undecided
Grammar	relative pronouns
Skills	reading: reading for specific information

[i]

National parks: America has about fifty national parks and over three hundred other protected areas such as national forests and national recreational areas. The national parks contain some of the most spectacular and unusual scenery in the United States. Six thousand full-time park rangers work in the parks, give lectures, organize campfire programmes in the evenings and take tourists on guided tours.

The National Park Service is a bureau of the Department of the Interior. It was founded in 1872 with the establishment of *Yellowstone National Park.* The area covered by the service includes not only the most extraordinary and spectacular scenic landscape in the United States, but also a large number of sites important either for their historic or prehistoric importance, scientific interest or superior recreational facilities.

Unit 10 · Human relationships

▬ Classroom A ▬▬▬▬▬▬▬▬▬▬▬▬▬▬▬▬▬

Students speculate about each other and create short factual texts. They also produce their own version of an English nursery rhyme.

◀ ▶

Functions	reacting to news	
	Good for him! / How terrible! / Isn't it awful? / That's fantastic! /	
	I'm sorry to hear that, but … / Lucky him!	
Skills	speaking:	verifying information;
		reacting and commenting on what others say;
		speculating about relationships
	writing:	writing a rhyme based on a given model
	reading:	reading questions as a stimulus for writing;
		reading nursery rhymes for enjoyment;
		reading rhymes created by other students
	listening:	listening to rhymes for enjoyment;
		listening to identify idiomatic phrases

Procedure

1 a Tell the students to write their name at the top of a sheet of paper, which they give to you. Distribute their papers making sure nobody gets his/her own name. Give the students enough time to read the twelve questions and write appropriate answers. Go round checking that the students are using the first person singular.

b Students work in pairs. As the papers are handed back suggest they verify the true statements and correct the false ones that have been written about them.

2 a Students work in pairs. Let them first read the three versions of the nursery rhyme silently. As they suggest which version is the original get them to justify their choice.

Original version: C

b With a partner get the students to create a new version of 'Solomon Grundy'. If they are daunted by the task, put the following frame on the board to show them they have very little to do to complete the text. They need only fill in one word for each line.

Solomon Grundy
_____ on Monday
_____ on Tuesday
_____ on Wednesday
_____ on Thursday
_____ on Friday
_____ on Saturday
_____ on Sunday
And that was the _____
Of Solomon Grundy

As they finish students should exchange their rhymes and try to read as many as possible. You could also do a wall display or get them to write on OHP transparencies.

c The students listen to the comments for each version, following the six sentences in their book on page 193, and work individually on the task. After they have filled in the comments get them to check with a partner and if necessary play the cassette a second time.

1. Good for him!
2. I'm sorry to hear that,
3. That's fantastic!
4. Isn't it awful?
5. Lucky him!
6. How terrible!

d Ask the students to note down their pieces of good and bad news. They read their statements to a partner who then comments. They can use the phrases from 2c if they wish. Collect some of the statements and comments on the board.

3 Put the students into pairs and let them explain to each other who they would like to have as neighbours and what sort of relationship they would like to have with these people. Do not allow the discussion to go on for too long. Get the class together and talk about neighbours they have or have had. There are likely to be some students who will have amusing anecdotes to tell about neighbours.

Home study A

1 Marriage makers puzzle
New topic   Physical characteristics

Students read a personal information file and decide which characteristics go with which person and make notes.

Vocabulary	amusing*, attractive, beard, build (n.), character*, curly*, eye, fair (adj.), fat (adj.), figure (n.), friendly, good-looking, height*, honest*, overweight, personality, sense of humour, shy*, similar, slightly*, thin
Skills	writing: writing personal statements
	reading: reading for specific information

2 What are you doing this evening?
New topic Invitations and excuses

Students practise responding to invitations and making excuses.

Functions	extending invitations and reacting
	Are you doing anything ...? / Are you free ...? / How about ...? /
	What about ...? / What are you doing ...? / Would you like to come
	out for ...? / I'm sorry, I'm travelling to London on Wednesday.
	expressing disappointment / regret
	How disappointing! / What a pity! / Oh, dear! / What a shame! / Oh, no!
Grammar	future: present continuous (arrangement)
Skills	listening: listening for specific information;
	listening and responding

i *Vet* (n.) is short for *veterinary surgeon.*

3 How about ...?
Extension Home study: Invitations and excuses

Students read a humorous article about being single and focus on invitations and vocabulary in this context.

Vocabulary	apologize, consider, date *(n.)*, desperate*, give up, herbal medicine*,
	hide *(v.)**, make fun of, settle
Functions	extending invitations and reacting
	How about ...? / I'm afraid ... / Would you like to ...? / That won't work. /
	What about ...? / Friday's out. / I'm sorry. / Sorry. I'm tied up ...
Skills	reading: reading for information;
	reading for specific information

Classroom B

Students read and talk about mixed marriages and exchange ideas and opinions.

◀ ▶

Skills	speaking:	giving descriptions from notes;
		giving descriptions using previously heard information
	writing:	note making as preparation for oral description;
		gap-filling to draw the students' attention to fillers
	reading:	reading questions to stimulate creative language;
		reading a text for information and to confirm speculations
		made about it
	listening:	focusing on detail to be able to reproduce what was heard

Procedure

1 **a** Get the students to look carefully at the pictures and choose one of them. Individually they answer the questions in note form.

Possible answer:
Bottom left picture: younger woman, older man
1. The woman's name is Emma.
2. She is Australian.
3. She is 26.
4. The man's name is John.
5. He is 54.
6. John is the manager of the Regal Theatre in Sydney and Emma is his secretary.
7. They met when Emma started working at the Regal.
8. They decided to stay together after six months of knowing each other.
9. Yes, they got married because the age gap is not important to them.
10. They live in a penthouse flat in the centre of Sydney.
11. Emma was born in Sydney and has always lived there. John is British and emigrated to Australia with his family when he was 12 years old.
12. Emma sometimes finds John a bit old-fashioned in his ways.
13. John gets annoyed when people mistake Emma for his daughter.

b Put the students into groups of three or four and ask them to listen to each other's descriptions. Students should not take notes.

c Get the students to regroup making sure there is only one member of the original groups in each of the new groups. Students then in turn tell one of the descriptions they have heard.

2 **a** Individually the students give their opinions marking the statements true or false. They can compare what they have marked with a partner and talk about the reasons for their choice.

b Students silently read the article *When the glamour has gone …* in the Student's Book on page 199 marking the statements true or false according to what the author says. If there are discrepancies between what they marked in 2a and what they found to be true or false according to the text in 2b, these points can be discussed with the whole class.

c The gap-filling serves as a test in text reconstruction, focusing on fillers. The more able students should manage to complete the sentences from memory. Encourage them to do as many sentences as possible without looking back at the text. They can then consult the text for any words that are still missing.

1. otherwise   2. so that   3. Although   4. because   5. Even though

Bring in some dice for the game next week (C-Block).

Home study B

1 Dear Fanny
Extension Classroom: Problems and advice (H4C/2)

Students read letters in an advice column and match them to the advice columnist's answers.

Vocabulary	angry, bother *(v.)*, disturb, drive s.o. crazy, gift*, guilty, ignore*, be obsessed with*, obviously, rudeness*, tired, tolerant*, upset *(adj.)**, warn, wonder *(v.)*
Functions	giving advice *You'd better (not) … / You should/shouldn't … / It's (not) up to you to …* talking about feelings *I'm completely fed up with … / It's driving us crazy. / I'm terribly angry with … / I feel guilty about … / I'm wondering what to do … / I'm extremely upset.*
Grammar	modal verbs: *had better* (advice/warning) *should* (advice)
Skills	reading: reading for information; reading for specific information

2 What do you think?
Extension Classroom: Agreeing and disagreeing (C8C/2)

Students listen to eight short dialogues and tick off phrases of agreement and disagreement as they hear them. They then group these phrases under headings and use them to state their own opinion.

Vocabulary	depend, engaged *(adj.)*, opinion, truth, (un)pleasant
Functions	agreeing and disagreeing *I disagree with you. In my opinion, … / That's true. / I'm not sure about that. I think it depends on … / That's rubbish! / I don't think you can say that. / That may be true in some cases, but … / Well, it depends. / You can say that again!*

3 Relationships
Extension Classroom: Talking about relationships

Students read through the songtext *Some Kind of Love* and fill in the missing words.

Vocabulary	heal*, thief, wheel *(n.)*, wound*
Skills	reading: reading for information; reading for specific information; reading for enjoyment

▬ Classroom C ▬▬▬▬▬▬▬▬▬▬▬▬▬▬▬▬▬▬▬▬▬▬▬

Students play a board game which revises elements from the previous ten units.

Procedure

Arrange the students in groups of four to five around the game in the book. Each group should have a die and each student a button, coin, or counter. The first student in each group throws the die and moves round the board according to the number thrown. He/she has to talk about the topic given in the square reached and should also be prepared to answer any questions relevant to the topic from others in the group. The second player followed by the third, fourth and fifth proceed in the same way.
The game is not competitive and the aim is to encourage the students to talk freely using knowledge they have acquired in the course in a relaxed, pressure-free atmosphere.

After about 30 minutes bring the students together for a formal or informal end-of-course feedback session.

☞ If this is the last lesson, you may want to talk to your students about how they can carry on learning English. You can also draw their attention to *Tips and books* in the Student's Book on page 296.

Remind your students of the crossword in the C-Block of the Home study section. Encourage them to do the crossword at home, perhaps together with another student if they wish.

The crossword recycles a number of words and phrases students have come across in *On Target*. It is therefore a kind of revision for the students as well as a nice means to round off the course.

Further activities

1 Practise spelling names and addresses

Ask the students to get a pencil and paper ready. They should then walk around the classroom and ask each person his/her name, address and phone number. Start them off by asking if they know what questions they need to ask and write them on the board or OHP for the weaker learners. You can join in on this activity. After this activity each learner will have a list of all the people in the class.

Examples:
1. Excuse me, what's your name?
2. Could you spell that, please?
3. And your address/telephone number?

2 Formal and informal introductions

Regroup the students by getting them to line up according to height or shoe size and then form groups of three. Ask them to practise introducing each other in a formal and an informal way using the language introduced in H1A/4. For other ways of regrouping students see the partner-finding activities on pages 128 to 133.

3 Discussion on reading texts

Before the students tackle the reading comprehension texts in the Home study section, it might be a good idea to have a short discussion on the purpose of reading comprehension exercises and what is expected of the students. Write the following statements on the board or OHP and get the students to decide which sentence best describes how they feel. You may want to have this discussion in the students' native language. Point out that there are different types of reading, compare them and collect examples of the students' reading experience in their native language.

1. I like to understand everything I read, even if I find it boring.
2. I am not happy until I understand every single word in a text.
3. I feel stupid if there are words I do not understand. I cannot just read over them.
4. I try to understand the main points of a text.
5. If I am really interested in a text, I will go back and look up words I think are important for me.

4 Writing personal letters

Get the students to put their names in a basket. Ask each student to take a name and write that person a short note thanking him/her for something.

5 Daily life vocabulary

In H1C/4 students have drawn two pie charts of their daily life. Use this as a warm-up activity. Collect the charts, mix them up and lay them out on tables or make a wall display. Students should walk around the room reading the different charts and see if they can guess which chart belongs to whom. Ask them to find the person whose pie chart is most like their own or most different.

Further activities

6 Starting a conversation

Get the students to think of two or three questions to start a conversation (remember: the weather is a good conversation starter; H1C/2) and write them on a card. You should go around the classroom and check the questions before the game begins. The students can then walk around the classroom, starting conversations with other students and noting down their different responses.

After the students have had a chance to gather responses, get them to sit in a circle and read out their own card and the response they liked best.

7 Day or night person?

Ask students to think of more questions for the quiz *Are you a morning or a night person?* (H2A/2) and write them on the board. Students interview each other asking the questions from the quiz and from the board. Get them to write five sentences about the student interviewed and report to the group. Find out how many night people there are in your class.

Examples:
1. Do you read the newspaper in the morning before work?
2. Do you listen to the radio in the morning?
3. Do you enjoy talking on the phone with friends in the evening?
4. Do you fall asleep in front of the TV or at the cinema when it gets too late?
5. When do you feel most tired?

8 Housework

In H2B/1d students were asked to write down jobs around the house that they like and do not like. Check to see that your students have completed the exercise and then try the following game.

Tell your students that you will write new vocabulary on the board after the game.

1. Students stand in a circle. You'll need a soft foam ball or a tennis ball. Teacher starts out by saying:
   I like playing with the children, but I hate doing the dishes.

2. Teacher throws ball to a student who then has to say something about himself/herself:
   I like cooking, but I don't like cleaning.

3. Student then throws the ball on to another student. This continues until all the students have had a chance to say what jobs around the house they like and dislike.

4. Teacher gets the ball from the last student and continues the game by reporting what someone else said:
   Jenny likes taking care of the plants, but she hates cleaning the bath.

5. Teacher then throws the ball on to Jenny. Jenny chooses someone new and reports:
   Inge likes cleaning windows, but she hates cooking lunch.
   She throws the ball on to Inge.

6. Continue like this until everyone has had a chance to speak. Students should help each other to remember what everyone has said.

9 Work routine

Tell your students to find a partner and get them all to look at the questions in the grid (H2C / 1c). Ask each student to interview at least three other students (other than the partner they usually work with) and note down their answers. Then ask them to go back to their partner and report what they have found out. If someone does not work, ask them to think of a job they would like to have and answer the questions for that job.

10 What's my line?

Let students play the job-guessing game in groups of four or five. One student thinks of a job and the others have to guess by asking questions that can be answered with *yes* or *no*.

11 What can you do there?

Ask students to bring some photos or postcards of a place they like to go on holiday. Students can also bring pictures from travel brochures. They show their photos/ postcards and pictures to the others who can then ask any questions they like.

12 Drawing by following instructions

Tell your students they should get ready to draw a picture. Then read the following instructions out loud.
Students should compare pictures afterwards. If there is time, get students to make up their own instructions in the same way and try them out with a partner.

1. Draw two trees. Draw one on the left and one in the middle of the paper.
2. Draw a house next to the tree on the right.
3. Draw a person between the two trees.
4. Draw a bird in the tree on the left.
5. Draw a girl looking out from behind the tree in the middle.
6. Draw some flowers in front of the house.

13 Discussion on listening comprehension

Listening to a foreign language can be very difficult for some students. Below are some things students often say about listening comprehension. Write the following sentences on the board or OHP and ask students to comment. Remind students that they are learning to understand people speaking English so they will be prepared when they meet a native speaker.

1. People on cassettes speak too fast and mumble. It's terrible!
2. If I meet someone in real life, I can watch their mouth, their face, etc. which helps me to understand what they say.
3. I hate it when I can't understand all of the words.
4. Why do we have to listen to native speakers talking naturally? It's too difficult. We can do that when we are more advanced.
5. I like listening to different people speaking English. It's the only way I'll learn to understand them.

Further activities

14 Interview

Students work in pairs. Get them to write down a few questions they would like to ask each other. If a student does not want to answer a question, he/she can say *pass*. After the students have interviewed each other, sit in a circle and let each student report about some interesting things they learned about each other.

15 What's the name of the town?

Ask students to write three or four sentences about a city or town without naming it. While students are writing you can go around correcting the texts. Then ask students to read their descriptions out loud. The others have to guess the name of the town or city being described.

Example:
It is a city in the east of the United States.
There is a famous statue there.
It is also known as the Big Apple.
Do you know the name of the city?
(New York)

16 Food vocabulary: odd one out

Students have completed H4A/3b. Get them to make up their own example of an *odd one out* and write it on the board or OHP. Ask the whole class to think of solutions.

17 Recipes for an end-of-semester cocktail party (Worksheet)

Photocopy the worksheet on page 118 and discuss vocabulary the week before your party. All the recipes can be made in class.

You will need:
a large jug (for the punch)
3 or 4 sharp knives
3 or 4 chopping boards
4 medium-sized bowls (for mixing dip and cheese ball)
2 plates (for the vegetables)
a few knives and spoons (for mixing and serving)
cups or glasses for the punch
serviettes

Get the students to volunteer to bring different ingredients and cooking utensils. Stress that everything will be done in class. If you want, you can substitute the *Hero Sandwich* in the Student's Book on page 91. This can also be made in class. Use this opportunity to speak English in a new informal situation.

18 What can't you do without?

Ask students to write down three things that they always have in their fridge. Collect the sheets of paper and spread them out where everyone can read them and get students to guess which sheet goes with which person.

19 In a restaurant. Describing food from your home country.
(Worksheet: role play)

Photocopy the worksheet on page 119. Ask students to bring menus from their home country to class. An alternative would be to get the students to write a list of typical foods from their area on the board or OHP. Divide the students up into groups of three. Students A and B are in a restaurant discussing what they would like to eat. Student C is the waiter/waitress who offers to help A and B by explaining the dishes on the menu. He/she then takes their order. Get students to change roles.

20 Vocabulary game

This is a guessing game to be played in groups. Get each student to think of a task (see below) and write it on a card. On the back of the card they should write the answers to their task.

Examples:
Name four things you can find in every village. (telephone box, houses, pub, shop)
Name five countries in southern Europe. (Italy, France, Spain, Portugal, Greece)

21 Mind maps

One way students can recycle vocabulary is to use mind maps, also known as vocabulary networks or word maps. The mind map method goes back to *Tony Buzan* who developed it in the seventies.
It is easier for students to remember words if they group them according to the meanings and associations they find for them.
A mind map, however, is not only a good method to recycle vocabulary, it is also invaluable as a prewriting activity. As such, it is important that the learner is given time to work on his/her mind map and to get feedback and comments from other learners. In doing so, new ideas and new words will be discovered which can be included later on in his/her written work.

There are different ways of drawing a mind map (see for example pages 92 and 95 in the Student's Book).

Divide students into groups of three and get them to make their own mind map for the subject area of FOOD. Give groups a chance to compare mind maps.

Suggest to the students that they make their own mind maps at home for other topics (e.g. people, daily life, places, …) and get them to compare mind maps in the next lesson. (You might want to give the students an OHP transparency and a pen.)

22 Interview

Students have completed a quiz at home and written two of their own questions in H5A/4b. Get students to make a class quiz by passing a piece of paper around so they can write down the questions they have thought of. Then copy the paper and hand it back to the students. (With more advanced students you may want to get groups to write their own quizzes.) Now give students time to interview each other. If there is time, you can ask students to report on any interesting experiences they heard about.

Further activities

23 Shopping

Get students to bring pictures of clothes or some magazines to class and ask them to cut out items of clothing. They can then set up shops and practise buying and selling using the dialogue from H5A/3.

24 My grandmother's suitcase

Ask students to bring an item or a piece of clothing they usually take on a trip. Alternatively, get students to draw a picture of one item they usually take on a trip. Ask students to sit in a circle. Student A says: *I packed my grandmother's suitcase and in it I put ...* (he/she names the item he/she brought and holds it up for everybody to see). Student B repeats the sentence, shows and names his/her item and repeats the previous item, too. The game goes on like this until all items have been shown and named. The last person has to name all the items. Students should be encouraged to help one another.

25 Talking on the phone

Get students to work in pairs and write their own dialogues using the telephone chart in H5B/2c. Let them read or act their dialogues out to the class.

26 Discussion on opening hours

Students have written five sentences giving their views on Sunday opening in H5C/2d. Get them to compare their views. Then write the following sentences on the board and ask students for their opinions. Students should use the expressions from H5C/2b.

1. Small shops should be allowed to stay open as long as they want to.
2. It's a good thing to have some shops open 24 hours a day.
3. Family businesses should be banned.
4. Every shop should stay open at least three evenings a week.
5. City offices should stay open in the afternoon and on at least one evening a week.

27 In an office (Worksheet)

Photocopy the worksheet on page 120. Get the students to write sentences about what Mike has done and what he hasn't done yet.

28 Places to visit in the Lake District (Worksheet)

Photocopy the worksheets on pages 120 and 121. Ask students to read about the places and answer the questions. This exercise can be done as a preview to H6A/3.

Key:

1. 5	2. 3	3. 1	4. 4	5. 2
6. 6	7. 1	8. 6	9. 1,5	10. longest
11. oldest	12. liveliest	13. 2, 3, 4, 6	14. 1,5	15. *own answer*

29 Holiday interview

Ask students to look back at the questions in H6B/4b. Ask each student to interview at least two other students and take notes. Afterwards get each student to report on another student's holiday.

30 Translate these sentences

Dictate the following sentences to the students. Then give them enough time to translate the sentences. Walk around and help if necessary. Finally, ask the students to read out their translations. The rest of the class can help with correction work.

1. At a party last night I met an old friend of mine.
2. I've been to New York twice.
3. I know you won't believe it, but yesterday I took a day off.
4. I was ill on holiday two years ago.
5. Did you travel to London last weekend?
6. I've never lived in the countryside, but I'd like to sometime.
7. I've already seen the latest musical in London.
8. Have you ever ridden on a camel?

31 Since our last English lesson ... (Worksheet)

Photocopy the worksheet on page 122 and get the students to tick only those statements that are true for them.
Students should then read their sentences to their partner giving him/her more details.

Examples:
Since our last English lesson I **have eaten** in a restaurant. Last Saturday I **ate** in the Turkish restaurant in town. The meal **was** very good.

Since our last English lesson I **have bought** new clothes. At the weekend I **went** to town and **bought** a pair of jeans and two sweatshirts.

32 Things you may say or hear on holiday (Worksheet)

Photocopy the worksheet on page 122. Ask students to read the sentences and tick what she/he has said or heard on holiday. Then students should get together with another partner and tell each other about the situations where they may have said or heard these things.

33 Remembering a journey

Put students into small groups and ask them to close their eyes and think of a trip they went on as a child. Give the students time to think back and then ask them to make notes on the following questions. Afterwards ask students to tell the others in the group about the journey they remembered.

1. What can you remember seeing on the trip?
2. What sounds can you remember hearing on the trip?
3. What smells can you remember?
4. Can you recall how something felt?
5. Can you remember the taste of something?

Further activities

34 Categories game (Worksheet)

Photocopy the worksheet on page 123. Students have three minutes to find a word that fits into each of the ten categories. Students should find words that start with a letter between *a* and *k*, for example. (In a good class you may want to give them only three letters, for example *c, d, e*.)

After three minutes, go around and ask each student which words he/she has written down for each category. If a student has written down a word that no one else has mentioned, then he/she scores a point. So for the game there are ten possible points. Most students find it interesting to hear what answers the others have thought of and especially enjoy this part of the game. You can discuss if answers are acceptable or not (or maybe even decide to give a bonus point for an especially funny answer).

35 A weekend in San Francisco (Worksheet: role play)

Photocopy the worksheets on pages 123 and 124.

Divide students up into groups of four. Then give each person in the group a different role card: A, B, C or D.

Ask students to look back in the Student's Book at the entertainment guide on page 156 and the map of San Francisco on page 126. Get them to plan a weekend together using the guide, the map and the language practised in H8A/4c.

36 The perfect weekend

Ask students to think about their perfect weekend. Tell them to write down five questions they would like to ask each other. Students should walk around and ask at least two people their questions. Then form a circle and give each student a chance to report on another student's idea of a perfect weekend. Make sure each person is reported on.

Possible questions:
1. Where would you go?
2. What would you do?
3. What would you have to eat?
4. What three things would you leave at home?
5. Who would you take along with you?

37 Treasure hunt

Get the students to draw a sketch of one room in their flat/house. Ask them to draw in the furniture and label it. Then ask them to hide something (e.g. a gold earring under the bed or a pen on a shelf in the wardrobe). Ask students to find a partner and guess where he/she has hidden the item.

If the hidden item has not been found after five guesses, the answer should be provided. Students should then change roles.

Example:
▲ I've hidden an earring.   ◆ Is it under the table?
                                         ◆ Is it on the floor in the right-hand corner?
                                         etc.

38 Protecting the environment

Put students into groups of three or five and ask them to write down at least three ideas
or suggestions on how to protect the environment. Then get students to exchange lists
with another group and discuss the ideas they received.
Finally, get the different groups to present the ideas first and then report back the
results of their discussions.

39 Who is it?

Get the students to write a short description of a famous person (alive or no longer
alive, e.g. a pop star, politician, actor/actress, etc.) on a card. Collect the cards and hand
them out again, making sure the students do not get their own card. They then read out
loud what it says on their card and the rest of the class guess who it might be.

40 Dear Fanny

Ask students to form pairs and write their own letter to Fanny stating a real or
imaginary problem. The teacher can go around correcting letters as they are being
written. Then, collect the letters and redistribute them. Get the pairs to write an
answer to the letter they receive. Ask pairs to read out the letters and replies and
then encourage students to put forward an alternative suggestion.

Photocopiable worksheets

Photocopiable worksheets for the following *further activities*:
17 (page 112), 19 (page 113), 27 (page 114), 28 (page 114), 31 (page 115), 32 (page 115),
34 (page 116) and 35 (page 116).

17 Recipes for an end-of-semester cocktail party

Champagne punch

Mix in a large jug:

1 bottle of champagne or
1/2 a bottle of mineral water
1 bottle of cherry juice
1 bottle of orange juice
1 bottle of ginger ale

Add:
ice cubes and slices of orange,
or other fruits of your choice

Raw vegetable dip

serves 6

Mix together in a bowl:

1 cup of sour cream
4 small gloves of garlic, crushed
1 teaspoon of onion, finely chopped
1 teaspoon of chopped parsley
2 tablespoons of chopped chives
a dash of Worcester sauce
a pinch of salt

Serve with raw vegetables cut into bite-sized pieces:
carrots, celery, mushrooms, cauliflower and peppers.

Curry-chutney cheese ball
serves 8

Mash together with a fork:

200 g of cream cheese (e.g. Philadelphia)
2 tablespoons of chutney
1 teaspoon of curry

Form a ball. Sprinkle 1/2 cup of chopped
almonds over it. Serve with crackers.

19 Role play: In a restaurant. Describing food from your home country.

Student A

You are visiting B. You can't understand the menu and you don't know any of the dishes. Ask your friend to explain what some of the dishes are and to recommend something to you. You like trying new foods, but there are some foods you don't like (e.g. meat).

Example:
Can you tell me what … is?
That sounds good. I like …
Hmmm. I'm not very fond of … What is …?

Student B

Imagine you are having dinner in a restaurant with an English-speaking friend. He/she asks you what the different dishes on the menu are. Explain to your guest what the dishes are made of and what they are like. Recommend something.

It's a/an	sweet/sour spicy/mild hot/cold alcoholic/non-alcoholic light/heavy creamy …-flavoured	dish dessert drink starter salad soup main dish	made with …

Example:
Why don't you try …? It's a speciality of this area.
I can recommend it!

Student C

You are the waiter/waitress in a restaurant. At one of your tables the customers are having a long discussion. Go over and see if you can help them. Take their order.

Example:
Good evening. Can I help you?
Yes, of course, it's a …
It's very good. / It's very popular with our guests.
Are you ready to order? What would you like to drink? / What would you like in the way of starters? / What kind of dressing would you like? / How would you like your meat? / Can I get you something else? / Would you like some coffee? / This is on the house.

Photocopiable worksheets

27   In an office

Mrs Adams works in an office. She has a young trainee, Mike, to help her. Every morning she gives him a list of things to do. Mike ticks off the things as he does them. During the day Mrs Adams checks what he has or hasn't done.
When Mrs Adams checks what Mike has done what does he say?

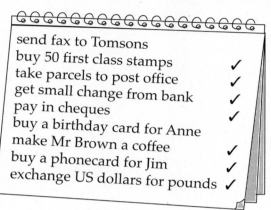

```
send fax to Tomsons
buy 50 first class stamps        ✓
take parcels to post office      ✓
get small change from bank       ✓
pay in cheques                   ✓
buy a birthday card for Anne
make Mr Brown a coffee           ✓
buy a phonecard for Jim          ✓
exchange US dollars for pounds   ✓
```

✂ -

28   Places to visit in the Lake District

Look at the descriptions of places to visit in the Lake District.

Where can you

1.   do all sorts of sports? _____

2.   find out a lot about the Lake District? _____

3.   have lunch or go to a folk concert? _____

4.   take a trip on an old steamboat? _____

5.   see some beautiful scenery without walking or driving? _____

6.   visit England's first round house? _____

Which places are

7.   closed all day Sunday? _____

8.   closed on Saturday? _____

9.   open all year? _____

Complete these sentences:

10. Windermere is England's _____ lake.

11. 'Dolly' is the _____ mechanically-powered boat in the world.

12. The Brewery Arts Centre is the _____ arts complex in the north.

What could you do or where could you go

13. on a sunny day? _____

14. on a rainy day? _____

15. Which of these places looks most interesting to you? _____

① Brewery Arts Centre, Kendal

Situated in the heart of Kendal stands a magnificent 150-year old brewery. The building has been extensively converted to become the liveliest arts complex in the north, presenting a continuous programme of exhibitions, theatre, folk, jazz, mime. Popular lunchtime restaurants and cosy Vats Bar.

OPENING TIMES:
Centre: Mon–Sat 09.00–23.00, Restaurant: 09.30–15.00, Vats Bar: 11.30–14.00 and 19.00–22.30 (23.00 Fri & Sat.). Tel. Kendal 25133.

HOW TO GET THERE:
Arts Centre and car park off Highgate – follow road signs to Brewery Arts Centre.

② Sealink's Windermere Pleasure Cruisers

There is no better way to enjoy Windermere than from the deck of a Sealink pleasure cruiser. It's the only way to really appreciate England's longest lake. Relax and enjoy 10.5 miles of water framed by mountains and woodland, from the Swan, Teal or Tern.

Opening Times: Daily service operates from Lakeside, Browness and Waterhead (Ambleside) Easter to September. Tel. Newby Bridge (0448) 31539.

How to get there: Choose from three piers – Lakeside, Browness and Waterhead

③ Brockhole National Park Centre near Windermere

Set in beautiful gardens and lakeside grounds the house contains lively permanent audio-visual exhibitions on all aspects of the Lake District. Regular slide presentations, terrace cafeteria, bookshop, nature trail, play area, summer launch trips and garden tours. Beatrix Potter Grotto and new "Living Lakeland" exhibitions. The perfect start to your lakeland holiday.

OPENING TIMES: Daily from 10.00 late March to early November.

HOW TO GET THERE: Tel. Windermere (09662) 2331. A591 between Windermere and Ambleside.

④ Windermere Steamboat Museum

Magnificent lakeside setting for a unique and historic collection of steam and motor boats, many afloat, under cover and in good working order, including 'Dolly' – the oldest mechanically powered boat in the world. Special party and family rates. Steam launch trips aboard Osprey (1902) subject to weather and availability.

Opening Times:
Open April to mid November inclusive from 10.00–17.00 daily. Sundays 14.00–17.00. Tel. Windermere (09662) 5565 for details.

How to get there:
The museum is situated on the lake shore 1/4 mile north of Browness on the A592.

⑤ South Lakeland Leisure Centre

Superb sports and entertainment facilities with swimming, squash, badminton, sauna/sunbeds, fitness unit, licensed bar and cafeteria. The centre also provides an ideal venue for many top class classical/light entertainment concerts each year. Come and visit us – we really do have something for everyone.

OPENING TIMES:
09.00–23.00 daily.
For exact times/details of facilities you are interested in, tel. Kendal 29777.

HOW TO GET THERE:
The Leisure Centre is situated in Burton Road on the south side of Kendal and motorists should follow the signs for A65. S.L.C.D., Leisure Service Dept.

⑥ Belle Isle, Windermere

Explore this 38 acre island in the centre of Lake Windermere and visit England's first round house built in 1774. Contents include portraits of the Curwens by Romney and specially designed Gillow furniture.

Guided tour of house four times daily at 11.15 a.m., 12.30, 2.30, and 4 p.m.
Open May 15th to September 15th, Sunday, Monday, Tuesday, Wednesday, Thursday. Covered motor boats run half hourly from Bowness Bay (opposite information centre) to the island from 10.15 a.m. to 3.45 p.m., returning up to 5 p.m. Charges which include return boat trip to island, or a short stay and guided tour of house; £2 per adult, children half price. Special rates for parties. Further enquiries please phone Windermere 3353.

31 Since our last English lesson …

Look at the following statements and tick those that are true for you. Read your sentences to your partner giving him / her more information or details.

Since our last English lesson …
1. I have eaten in a restaurant. ☐
2. I have done some sport. ☐
3. I have seen a good film. ☐
4. I have got annoyed about something. ☐
5. I have read an interesting article. ☐
6. I have bought new clothes. ☐
7. I have written a letter. ☐
8. I have complained about something. ☐
9. I have been to the bank. ☐
10. I have been to the post office. ☐

✂ —

32 Things you may say or hear on holiday

This is a list of things people may have said or heard when they were on holiday.
Tick the ones that you have said or heard. Can you remember the situation?
Tell your partner about it.

1. I shouldn't have brought so much junk with me. I don't need half this stuff. ☐
2. I wish I'd brought more money. ☐
3. We'll never stay here again! ☐
4. I should have brought some warmer clothing. I didn't know it would be this cold. ☐
5. I should have brought some lighter clothing. I didn't know it would be this hot. ☐
6. I wish we had restaurants like this at home! ☐
7. Do you know how you're supposed to eat this? ☐
8. Don't these people believe in street signs? ☐
9. You can get that for half the price at home! ☐
10. This is such a beautiful place. I'd love to live here. ☐
11. It was nice meeting you. Come and see us when you are in … (name of your town) ☐
12. I never thought a map could be so confusing. I've never been this lost in my life. ☐
13. They drive like maniacs here! ☐
14. It's a good thing you remembered to bring this along! ☐
15. Remind me to get some postcards tomorrow. ☐
16. This is a real tourist trap. I can't imagine why … (name of a friend) told us to come here. ☐
17. I wish all these other people had stayed at home. ☐
18. We didn't come all this way for you to order a hamburger. ☐
19. I'll never go on this type of holiday again! ☐
20. I can't believe it's already time to go home. ☐
21. We still haven't written any postcards. ☐
22. What's the first thing you're going to do when you get home? ☐
23. Luckily, I didn't need this. ☐
24. It's changed a lot since we were here last. ☐

34 Categories game

You have three minutes to think of a word that starts with a letter between *a* and *k* and which fits into the ten categories below.

1. Something you take on a trip.   _____

2. An animal that is larger than a cat.   _____

3. Clothing you wear in cold weather.   _____

4. Something you might see at an airport. _____

5. Something that has wheels.   _____

6. A colour.   _____

7. A word describing weather.   _____

8. Something you might see near the sea. _____

9. Something you do not like while you are on holiday. _____

10. A drink.   _____

- -

35 Role play: A weekend in San Francisco

A The vegetarian people-watcher

You have won a weekend trip with three other people to San Francisco. You all arrive on Friday afternoon at the airport and go to your hotel. It's a very expensive hotel near Fisherman's Wharf. Now you must plan with the others what you are going to do together from Friday evening until Sunday evening when your plane leaves at 5 p.m.

Plan the weekend but keep in mind that you love going to the theatre. You are a vegetarian who likes to go to seafood restaurants. You also want to go to the Japanese Tea Garden for tea and you are interested in spending at least three hours shopping in the department stores at Union Square. You love people-watching, and would like to spend some time just walking around the Fisherman's Wharf area.

Use the Entertainment Guide on page 156 and the map of San Francisco on page 126.
Look at H8A/4c for useful language.

B The quiet nature lover

You have won a weekend trip with three other people to San Francisco. You all arrive on Friday afternoon at the airport and go to your hotel. It's a very expensive hotel near Fisherman's Wharf. Now you must plan with the others what you are going to do together from Friday evening until Sunday evening when your plane leaves at 5 p.m.

Plan the weekend but keep in mind that you hate strange foods and will absolutely refuse to go anywhere that only serves foreign foods. Otherwise, you like listening to jazz or going to a good documentary film. You would also like to have dinner at the Cliff House, take a walk on the beach and enjoy the sunset. You want to spend time walking around North Beach and you insist on going to the aquarium at the natural history museum in Golden Gate Park.

Use the Entertainment Guide on page 156 and the map of San Francisco on page 126.
Look at H8A/4c for useful language.

C The adventurous Mexican food lover

You have won a weekend trip with three other people to San Francisco. You all arrive on Friday afternoon at the airport and go to your hotel. It's a very expensive hotel near Fisherman's Wharf. Now you must plan with the others what you are going to do together from Friday evening until Sunday evening when your plane leaves at 5 p.m.

You love all kinds of food, especially Mexican food. You can't stand classical music or rock concerts, but don't mind jazz or country music. You are very keen on Diane Keaton and would like to see her in a film. You are also interested in walking over the Golden Gate Bridge. You have always wanted to do this. You would like to go to Chinatown and look around the shops. Don't forget, you want to ride on a cable car, too.

Use the Entertainment Guide on page 156 and the map of San Francisco on page 126.
Look at H8A/4c for useful language.

D The jogger

You have won a weekend trip with three other people to San Francisco. You all arrive on Friday afternoon at the airport and go to your hotel. It's a very expensive hotel near Fisherman's Wharf. Now you must plan with the others what you are going to do together from Friday evening until Sunday evening when your plane leaves at 5 p.m.

You enjoy going out for interesting meals at exotic restaurants. You have heard that China-town has some good restaurants and you would like to look around the shops there for a present for your mother's birthday. You like listening to music, especially Country music. You don't mind going to the cinema, but you can't stand science-fiction films. You want to go for a jog in Golden Gate Park and visit the museum in the Palace of the Legion of Honor. You also think it would be fun to walk around the city at night and walk down Lombard Street.

Use the Entertainment Guide on page 156 and the map of San Francisco on page 126.
Look at H8A/4c for useful language.

Classroom activities

Photocopiable material for Classroom handouts.

C1B/1 (Student's Book, page 18)

1.	You hear	You say
	Start	A H J
	E G S	X L M
	Z T X	F N E
	F H U	B I W

2.	You hear	You say
	S V W	O Y I
	B P D	R U A
	O D H	P D G
	U N F	Z E J

3.	You hear	You say
	A H J	L M P
	M E C	Z T X
	B I W	O D H
	Z E J	Stop

4.	You hear	You say
	O Y I	E G S
	R U A	M E C
	F N E	Y O T
	I J G	U N F

5.	You hear	You say
	L M P	S V W
	X L M	B P D
	Y O T	F H U
	P D G	I J G

Classroom activities

C7C/1 (Student's Book, page 144)

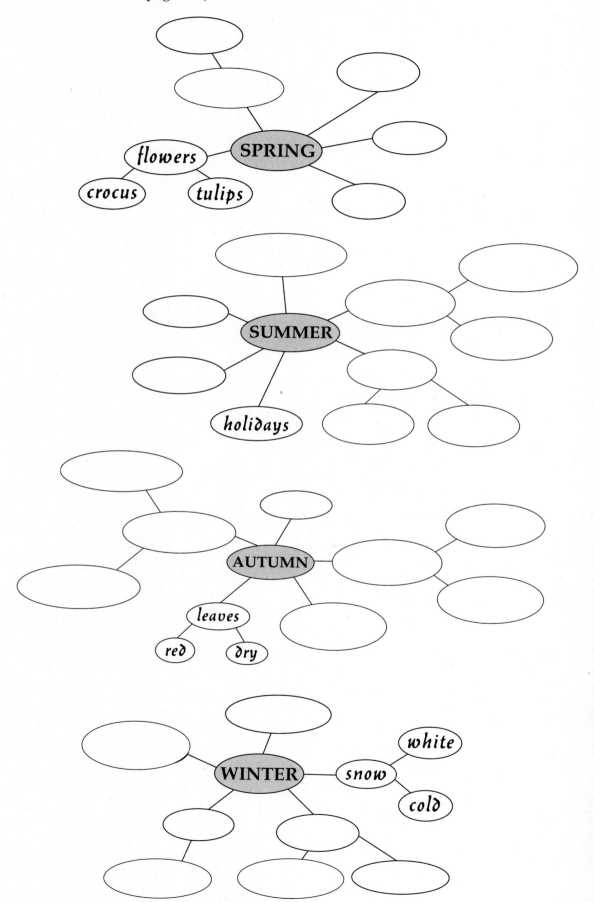

© Ernst Klett Verlag für Wissen und Bildung GmbH, Stuttgart 1994. Alle Rechte vorbehalten. (Vervielfältigung zum Unterrichtsgebrauch gestattet.)

FACED WITH a health service devoted to treating illness rather than preventing it, people are buying their own preventive medicine. Dietary supplements such as vitamins and minerals, once the preserve of cranks, have moved into the mainstream, writes David Nicholson-Lord.

Half of the population will take a supplement at some time, while sales have increased by an estimated 45 per cent over the past four years, making dietary supplements the biggest and fastest-growing sector of health products sold over the counter, according to a report published yesterday.

Based on a survey of 3,500 customers of Boots, the report stated that people take the supplements to prevent illness. According to Dr Ann Walker, a nutritionist from Reading University, research will increasingly demonstrate that to achieve "optimal" health, intakes of certain vitamins and minerals must be higher than those now recommended.

Recent studies have shown that higher than average intakes of vitamins C and E, for example, may help to maintain a healthy heart and prevent a wide range of degenerative diseases. The amount of fruit and vegetables recommended to prevent chronic disease – five or six servings a day – may represent too drastic a change in diet for many people, making dietary supplements a likely alternative.

A GUNMAN killed a man who tried to tackle him after he wounded two police officers outside a nightclub in Sheffield, writes Will Bennett.

The bravery of the dead man, Shaun Hadley, 23, a building labourer, from Dronfield, near Sheffield, was praised by police and his family yesterday. He was waiting to go into Josephine's nightclub late on Friday when the shooting occurred. A man stopped for questioning by a police officer produced a sawn-off shotgun and fired it through the window of a patrol car before running towards the nightclub.

Chief Superintendent Michael Burdiss said: "There was an attempt to detain the man and during this the shotgun was fired. Shaun Hadley was struck in the chest and died from his injuries."

Mr Hadley's uncle, Bill Corbett, said: "He was trying to be helpful in a dangerous situation, which has tragically cost him his life. He was the sort of man who would go in and help people."

Ch Supt Burdiss said one officer in the car, PC Graham Saunders, was saved by the personal radio on his shoulder which deflected some of the shotgun pellets. PC Saunders, who was hit in the chest, and his colleague PC Gary Littler, who was hit in the hand, were released from hospital after treatment.

A man is being questioned about the incident.

B

THE MAXIMUM jail sentence is to be doubled for the large majority of teenage offenders. Ministers have agreed to lift it from one year to two for juveniles who commit relatively minor crimes – a decision which prison reformers describe as cruel and pointless.

The present one-year maximum applies to all 15 to 17-year-olds in Prison Service young offender institutions, apart from those convicted of murder, rape and other very serious offences.

The decision was forced on the Home Office by the rushed response of Kenneth Clarke, when he was Home Secretary, to public concern about crime.

Mr Clarke promised in March to take persistent young offenders aged between 12 and 15 away from local authority care and put them in secure detention centres. Children who committed three or more offences would be given a maximum sentence of two years. The Bill to authorise the centres is due to go before the Commons in the autumn.

But civil servants noticed that the measure would create an absurdity: the maximum sentence for 12-year-olds would be one year longer than for 16-year-olds.

A Home Office review is still in progress but sources say the anomaly is certain to be resolved by raising the maximum for young people aged 15 to 17.

By Nick Cohen

Ministers have also looked at the minimum age of criminal responsibility in England and Wales – beneath which children cannot be charged. They considered lowering it from 10 to eight, bringing it into line with Scotland. But the Home Office seems to have rejected the idea.

However, the list of serious crimes carrying long jail sentences for the young may be extended.

Prison campaigners oppose the plans for longer sentences. Stephen Shaw, director of the Prison Reform Trust said: "Doubling the maximum penalty for teenagers who commit minor offences will inevitably lead to more children spending longer behind bars in these benighted institutions. Magistrates are bound to make use of the increased sentencing powers, particularly when the political lead is to follow the ineffective, cruel and pointless policy of locking teenagers up."

Paul Cavadino, spokesman for the National Association for the Care and Resettlement of Offenders, said that between 70 and 80 per cent of teenagers offend again on release. "It is very sad that this country is once again drifting into discredited and bankrupt policies," he said.

Source: The Independent

Partner-finding activities

1 British and American English
Match the British word with the American word.

biscuit	cookie	chemist's	drugstore
chips	French fries	film	movie
holiday	vacation	lift	elevator
motorway	freeway	pavement	sidewalk
petrol	gas	sweets	candy
toilet	restroom	town centre	downtown
trousers	pants	underground	subway

2 Proverbs

Match the beginning of the proverb with the correct ending.

A stitch in time	saves nine.	Actions speak	louder than words.
An apple a day	keeps the doctor away.	Better late	than never.
Don't count your chickens	before they're hatched.	Every cloud	has a silver lining.
Home is	where the heart is.	Make hay	while the sun shines.
Prevention is	better than cure.	The early bird	catches the worm.
Too many cooks	spoil the broth.	Two heads	are better than one.
You can't have your cake	and eat it!	You can't teach	an old dog new tricks.

Partner-finding activities

3 Similes

Match the adjective with the correct noun.

Blind	as a bat.	Busy	as a bee.
Colder	than ice.	Cool	as a cucumber.
Dead	as a doornail.	Free	as a bird.
Nuttier	than a fruitcake.	Sly	as a fox.
Snug	as a bug in a rug.	Straight	as an arrow.
Strong	as an ox.	Stubborn	as a mule.
Thin	as a rake.	Warm	as toast.

4 Compound words

Match the first half of the word with the second half. (The first half of the word is capitalized.)

Air	line	Bath	room
Flower	pot	Foot	ball
Head	ache	House	wife
Land	lady	Motor	way
News	paper	Sea	side
Sales	woman	Sun	rise
Suit	case	Tooth	brush

5 Word partners

Find the correct partner for the phrases.

aunt and	uncle	bread and	butter
brother and	sister	cat and	dog
gold and	silver	house and	home
king and	queen	knife and	fork
night and	day	salt and	pepper
shoes and	socks	soap and	water
thunder and	lightning	war and	peace